ESSAYS IN MALTESE LEGAL HISTORY

AND COMPARATIVE LAW

VOLUME 1

Essays in Maltese Legal History and Comparative Law

VOLUME 1

Mark A. Sammut

Whitelocke
PUBLICATIONS

OXFORD NEW YORK LUXEMBOURG

Published by
WHITELOCKE PUBLICATIONS LIMITED
Oxford, United Kingdom
www.whitelockepublications.com
contact@whitelockepublications.com

Whitelocke Publications Limited was founded with
the objective of furthering legal research and scholarship
by publishing in

OXFORD NEW YORK LUXEMBOURG

Whitelocke®
PUBLICATIONS

"Publishers of Intelligent Books" © 2017 Whitelocke Publications Limited
WHITELOCKE PUBLICATIONS LIMITED
focuses on legal publishing.
Sir Bulstrode Whitelocke (6 August 1605 – 28 July 1675)
was an English lawyer, writer, parliamentarian,
and Lord Keeper of the Great Seal of England.

Whitelocke Publications®
is a registered trademark of Whitelocke Publications Limited

Published in the United Kingdom by Whitelocke Publications Limited

First published in 2016 by Russell Square Publishing Limited

Published in 2017 by Whitelocke Publications Limited

British Library Cataloguing in Publication Data
Data Available

Typeset by Kotba-Argo Limited, Malta
Printed in the United Kingdom

ISBN: 978-1-912142-01-9

The painting on the cover,
View of the Grand Harbour by Giorgio Pullicino (1779-1852),
is appearing courtesy of Heritage Malta ©.

To
the President of the Constitutional Court
of the Republic of Italy

Paolo Grossi

Professor, Judge and Friend
in history of law, the Master

I think I've been guilty of being at the same time trivial and obscure. So one can't worry about this at a personal level. What is more encouraging is that I think one can find similar criticisms made with respect to most other disciplines, both by people outside them and, most interestingly perhaps, by people within them.

– Patrick Glenn

"Comparative Law: Problems and Prospects"
in 26 *American University International Law Review* 941 (2011)

ESSAYS IN MALTESE LEGAL HISTORY

AND COMPARATIVE LAW

VOLUME 1

Contents

About the author:

Mark A. Sammut, a member of the Royal Historical Society, the European Society for Comparative Legal History, and of the Malta Historical Society, studied law and translation studies at the University of Malta (LL.D., M.Jur. (*summa cum laude*), M.A.), Western European legal history at the University of London (LL.M.), and historical sociology at the London School of Economics.

He has written *A Short History of Latvia/L-Istorja tal-Latvja fil-Qosor* (Malta, 2004), co-written *Il-Liġi, il-Morali, u r-Raġuni* (*Law, Morality and Reason*) with Professor Giuseppe Mifsud Bonnici, former European Court of Human Rights Judge and former Chief Justice of Malta, (iusmelitae, Malta, 2008), contributed to *The Mediterranean Region: Different Perspectives, Common Objectives* (ed. P. Quercia, Ministry of Defence, Italy, 2010), written *The Law of Consular Relations* (XPL, UK, 2010), edited and co-authored *Malta at the European Court of Human Rights 1987-2012*, with M[e] Patrick Cuignet and Dr David A. Borg, with contributions by Prof. Kevin Aquilina, Dean of the Faculty of Laws of the University of Malta, Dr Giovanni Bonello, former Judge of the European Court of Human Rights, and Dr Therese Comodini Cachia, human rights lawyer and Member of the European Parliament (iusmelitae, Malta, 2012), and written *L-Aqwa fl-Ewropa. Il-Panama Papers u l-Poter* (Malta, 2016), a political commentary.

The opinions expressed in this book belong only to the author.

Foreword

by Prof. Dr. **Raymond Mangion**
B.A., B.A. (Hons), M.A., LL.D. (Melit.), D.Phil. (Oxon.)
Professor of Legal History & Methodology
Head of Department, Legal History & Methodology
Faculty of Laws, University of Malta

I HAVE BEEN asked by Mark A. Sammut, and have accepted with honour and pleasure his kind invitation, to pen some comments on the present collection of essays under his signature.

The primary and ultimate question that shall be posed by considering at face value such compilation is whether it is useful to research and study, let alone publish, the subject of legal history.

Legal history, often wrongly identified with legislative history (which is only one branch of it, another ramification would be judicial history), has been taught within the Faculty of Laws at the University of Malta since 1870 when Dr Niccolò Crescimanno, from Corleone, Sicily, was appointed as the first lecturer on History of Legislation in England and Malta. The validity of the subject's teaching at a tertiary level was at one time questioned when the issue was raised as to whether it was a theme worthy of academic research and study of its own. The subject of legal history ceased forming part of the syllabus and curriculum of research and study within the Faculty of Laws of the University of Malta in the 1980s soon after Professor Hugh Harding retired from the post. Fortunately enough, it was re-introduced as part of reforms to the structure of the course of laws in 1994. The relevant Department under the designation of Legal History and Legal Methodology was formally set up in 2012.

Legal History is neither exclusively the subject of Law nor exclusively the subject of History. It is both, together and altogether. It is a *sui generis* combination of law and history. It is academically as much humanistic as the two subjects severally treated and independently of each other. On the one hand, it is a subject where law has to be focused within a historical context. It is the research and study of law around which history is to rotate. On the other hand, it is the research and study of history seen from the perspective of law as a concept and instrument along the course of human development throughout the ages. It is history envisaged as a series and assemblage of persons and events taking place down the centuries under the influence of law in all its variants, namely legislation, court judgments, customs, jurists as well as language.

Mark A. Sammut has by his collection of essays composed between 2011 and 2015 demonstrated that legal history – and comparative law at that – is more than necessary. Legal history delves into the foundations of a country's institutions not only to track down their origins but to point out sources for a better application and interpretation of present rules and relationships at all strata of a community. Legal history makes the historian pay more attention and give more accuracy to the building up and piecing together of the annals of the past because he has to tell his story by complying as strictly as possible with the law and its language as they developed and existed over the years – and in many a situation as they still develop and exist. Otherwise, the legal historian who misses the law in retrospect, as a historical document, would be like the lawyer who ignores the obtaining law.

It is said that a man is a historian – and is able to recount facts of the past – if he is so born, especially if he is endowed with an unusual memory to store dates and facts. It is also said that a man is never born a lawyer; he has to research and study to learn the ropes, namely the application and enforcement of rules. Whereas the distinction between fact and law is ancient and classical, legal history is correctly and academically a discipline that requires the scholar to be systematically trained in both law and history. The legal historian has, of course, to focus on law within a historical context, as a state of fact of the past. However, he has to do so perhaps with more chronological precision than any other historian because he has to refer to law not only as a manuscript or document but as part of a structure while at the same time he has to indicate the extent of its role and effects on society.

Dr Sammut surveys by way of his first essay the judicial importation into Maltese Law of Italian private law solutions and its implications. Malta became constitutionally part of British sovereignty in 1814 in terms of the Paris Treaty, by voluntary cession of the Maltese pursuant to a Declaration of Rights in 1802 and British acceptance in line with *ad hoc* Instructions in 1813.

Juridically, Maltese private substantive and procedural laws continued to form part of the continental tradition. The Maltese Civil Code (1868/1873) retained the same basis of its Italian counterpart (1865) that had ultimately been modelled on the *Code Napoléon* (1804). The fount of Maltese law generally remained Italian judgments and Italian authors.

However, it is not wise at all to presume that the Italian and Maltese Civil Codes always say the same thing. Sir Adriano Dingli not only consulted the provisions of other leading continental Codes and particularly the Code of Louisiana, and treatises of text-writers of repute, but made interpolations to incorporate autochthonous or indigenous praxes.

Moreover, Dr Sammut draws the attention of his reader, and rightly so, that the Italian Civil Law system had a break with the past when the Italian legislator enacted and promulgated a new Civil Code (1942) and that the Maltese courts were dragged by the mentality to follow also the new, post-1942 Italian system, including Italian judgments and authors.

In point of fact, the new Italian Civil Code of 1942 distinguished between "rescission" and "simulation" of contracts under two separate chapters as opposed to its antecedent, the now defunct Italian Civil Code (1865), and to the hitherto extant Maltese Civil Code (1868/1873). Post-1942 Maltese court judgments are probative evidence that they are citing post-1942 Italian sources and judgments to the extent of treating "simulation" as a concept of its own.

Since Parliament is the sole legislative body of the Maltese State, judicial importation of legal principles from foreign judgments when the legislative bases are not identical obviously means that the Maltese Courts are overstepping their constitutional jurisdiction. By importing the rules contained in the legislation of another sovereign State which have no analogy in Maltese law, the

Maltese Courts are acting as a sovereign legislator. This is clearly against the Constitution which states that Parliament may pass laws, and with regard to the Courts it refers to the ordinary law, but there is no ordinary law which empowers the Courts to make law.

Next, Dr Sammut embarks on historical facts and myths surrounding the Criminal Code of Malta. He refers to what has been taught and written as follows: the Criminal Code (1854) in Malta had many of its substantive institutes and titles based on former municipal legislation. It took over thirty years to compile following many drafts, changes, discussions and suspensions, and was modelled on the taxonomic framework that was typical to continental codifications. It also successfully incorporated the relevant procedures in another part that was more Anglo-Saxon in approach. The Criminal Code had, however, one major problem that no criminal law expert could solve at the time. How could its redactors and revisers cope with the humanitarian movement of the epoch that was faster than them? The Criminal Code was so enacted, promulgated and brought into effect because the idea of nineteenth century codification, the fruition of the Enlightenment of the previous one hundred years, was meant to render more "sacred" legislation. Yet, barely had the Criminal Code been brought to bear when the Council of Government in Malta started resorting to a series of amendments and substitutions to soften its penal provisions in consequence of the then influx and infiltration of humanitarianism.

Dr Sammut draws the attention of his reader that the story of the Criminal Code in Malta was written subject to imperialist or neo-colonialist ideology and that it was, especially in relation to capital punishment and the scale of penalties in general, not as liberal as it has been thought to be. He appeals to his reader to review Maltese legal history, particularly the history of the Criminal Code, through Malta's and the Maltese's own perspective. Dr Sammut is more than correct so long as he refers to the pre-codification period when Mr Andrew Jameson, a Scottish Sheriff, asked by the British authorities to betake himself to Malta to be able to eke out a living, wielded appreciable clout on the crafting of the Criminal Code. The author's brilliant analysis is avowed by an uninterrupted series of legislative amendments of a humanitarian character to the Code's penal sections that the Council of Government implemented under the insistence of the local representatives soon after the original promulgation in 1854.

Dr Sammut entitles his third essay "Medieval (Legal) Beasts in our Midst? A Terminological *Ad Fontes* Look at the Dissolution of Contracts under Maltese Law." He picks up and compares the French two words "*résolution*" and "*résiliation*" which linguistically may have the same meaning but not legally. He admirably does so to investigate whether a norm depends on the language used or on the statutory idea behind the written precept. *Résolution* has, indeed, to do with the termination of an actual obligation whereas *résiliation* deals with the breach and end of a promise or future obligation. However, the Maltese Civil Code (1868) and its Italian counterpart (1865) use almost exclusively the term "dissolution", while the Maltese courts and Maltese doctrine, once again like the Italian authors, employ a threefold terminology words - "dissolution, "*résolution*" and "*résiliation*" interchangeably. The author sieves a number of Maltese cases to come to the conclusion that the Maltese courts follow the Italian pattern as far as the triadic nomenclature is concerned. Dr Sammut humbly declares that he is not a professional linguist and that his knowledge of legal history is limited to internal Western European Legal History. In reality, he is more than knowledgeable and adroit at handling legal history etymologically and linguistically and his blending them is marvellous as he amply shows by virtue of his third and fourth essay. He is surely in Malta a leader in the history of legal language.

Finally, Dr Sammut devotes his fourth essay to the obscure term "*midheb*" in Vassalli's *Lexicon* (1796) and its possible usefulness for the legal historian. He names his essay "Latin Wine Decanted into a Semitic Carafe...". Vassalli (1764-1829), the Father of the Maltese tongue, defines "*midheb*" (from Arabic "dahab", namely "to go" or "to follow") by translating it in Latin: "*lex propria & privata; hinc Lex & usus nationis: ritus*". Dr Sammut was led to report about the word in question because it did not feature in a previous known dictionary in manuscript form by De Soldanis (1750) as it had gone into desuetude and had survived only on the strength of lingering memory, and was left out by other lexicographers for almost 180 years after 1796. Unfortunately, Mr Erin Serracino Inglott and Professor Ġużè Aquilina reproduced it erratically in 1977 and 1990 because they simply connected its derivation from "*deheb*" (i.e. gold). Dr Sammut states that "*midheb*" is a variant equivalent to the Arabic "madhab" and had been, more or less, a general term for a whole legal system (that had obtained in Malta). Dr Sammut dissects the phrase in Latin as "the territorial/public law" (i.e. State-individual law) (*lex propria*) and "private law" (i.e. individual-individual law) (*lex privata*), hence "*Lex and usus nationis*" as "the law of the Prince and custom of the people" or "*ritu*" as "the social law in general". The author concludes that the terms "*midheb*" and "madhhab" are conceptually similar and so the Maltese term could be a classical instance of a fusion between the two cultures even if the domestic notion is to be viewed within a Christian-European while the Arabic one in an Islamic context. In brief, the word "*midheb*" is equivalent to "*ritu*" meaning the law that society follows, social law in general.

Dr Sammut regales his reader with four essays. The first has to do with the branch of judicial and juristic history, exactly with the extent of the nexus between Italians judgments and authors on one side, and Maltese law on the other side, particularly in the nineteenth century. The second turns around the long-drawn-out pre-codification period of the criminal laws of Malta. The third and fourth are more an exercise on the history of legal language - another important area of legal history that has never been tapped.

Dr Sammut more than vindicates that research and study of legal history is needed in varied ways. Plaudits to him for his innovative tackling of aspects of Maltese legal history characterised by extraordinary intuitions and conclusions.

Acknowledgements

NOT FAR FROM the entrance to the Vatican Museums in Rome, there is a second-hand bookshop next door to a *gelateria* and a musical instrument shop. Or at least, there used to be in 2003. It was there and in that year that my passion for legal history was conceived. On the basement level of that bookshop, while browsing the books on the shelves, I caught a glimpse of a yellow cover out of the corner of my eye. For the Italians, a yellow cover usually denotes a thriller. They actually call such novels, *gialli*, "yellows". But this was not a normal *giallo*. This was Paolo Grossi's *L'Ordine Giuridico Medievale* (*The Medieval Legal Order*), a book published in 1995 which every law student in Italy is supposed to have read but which is virtually unknown in my native Malta.

Upon coming back to Malta, I plunged into it and literally couldn't put it down. It was indeed written like a *giallo*. In the hands of a lesser author it might have turned out to be a drab book, arcane and obscure. But in Professor Grossi's hands, the history of medieval law comes to life – mostly because he uses a literary style which simply enchants you while employing medieval law as an excuse to explain modern, positivist law. It therefore encompasses that perfect marriage between history and theory of law. I couldn't help falling in love with both book and subject. The following year I flew to Florence appositely to ask him to sign it for me. I met him again two more times, in 2010 and 2014, by which time he had been elected Judge of the Constitutional Court. During this third visit, he took me to what he calls his *cascina*, his country house, where he spends days strolling up and down his large, tiered garden, and in the guest room I noticed a collection of Agatha Christie's *Poirot*. I turned toward him and said, "So I was right to claim that your style is thriller-like!" He replied with a kind, knowing smile and told me that he was happy that I had recognised in him not only the jurist but also the man of letters.

Out of this admiration for and friendship with Paolo Grossi was born my commitment toward legal history. From a simple intellectual passion, it became something deeper. I decided to study it systematically and enrolled at the University of London which offers an excellent course in Western European Legal History, organised by ADE Lewis, Professor of Comparative Legal History at University College London. He later revealed to me that he in turn had been a student of my Civil Law Professor, JM Ganado, when Ganado taught Roman Law as a young scholar at London.

In the meantime, my collection of history of law books had taken a life of its own and was growing like urban sprawl, grabbing more space in my medium-sized apartment. I kept buying unusual books, mostly in Italian and French, but also in English. In a fit of friendly banter, a one-time Professor at the University of London, once pulled my leg when I showed him one of my books, an Italian publication on Græco-Roman private law in Sicily. "They published ten copies," he teased me. "Nine they gave to the author and his family. The tenth, *you* bought!"

The more books I bought, the more the wish to start writing about this subject took hold of me. Mesmerised by Grossi's ideas on the important historical moment represented by 1789 – but not only Grossi's, also Natalino Irti's, Michel Villey's, JL Halperin's, and also Randall Lesaffer's – I found a channel to express the many impressions I had been accumulating throughout my life. Somehow it seemed as if my existence had only been the gathering of momentum for that watershed moment when I would at long last understand that history of law was my vocation. All of my life, I had listened to my father (a public thinker, among other things) preaching about the French Revolution, about which he wrote a book on the occasion of the bicentenary and numerous newspaper articles over the years. In my family's sitting room there are a few family photos on the fireplace, like in all normal sitting rooms. But then the rest of the room seems inspired by Thomas Carlyle: images of Napoleon Bonaparte and Jean-Jacques Rousseau, statuettes of Pericles and Solon ...

So when I met Randall Lesaffer, Professor at the Montesquieu School of Law at Tilburg University, in the Netherlands, my intuition told me that I had met a kindred soul. Dining, we spoke of Herodotus and the story of Croesus and Solon ... and the *Ancien Régime* and the Age of Codification ... His important work, published by Cambridge University Press, *European Legal History: A cultural and political perspective*, seemed to me natural – that was the only way to approach this subject, by combining culture, politics, and law. So I understood that, though we might be few, there is a brotherhood thinly spread over many countries engaged in the quest to determine whether we are historians or lawyers. Lesaffer seems to have solved the conundrum.

But so has also Raymond Mangion, Professor of History of Legislation at the University of Malta, who had started his academic career by studying history and then went on to study law and finally combined the two. He seems not to be troubled too much by this issue, as he has probably integrated the two worldviews, the historian's and the lawyer's, into peaceful and meaningful co-existence within him. This self-assuredness in Professor Mangion's *forma mentis* strikes me, deeply. It seems to give the right answer to many a soul-searching question.

So all these people combined have catalysed my desire to write on legal history.

An inveterate and incurable itch for writing besets many and grows old in their sick hearts. In my case, I do not think it grew old. Before embarking on the writing of legal history, I had already co-written a book with former Judge of the European Court of Human Rights and former President of the Constitutional Court and Court of Appeal of Malta, Professor Giuseppe Mifsud Bonnici. It was on philosophy of law[1] and

1 Despite its brevity and form, in *Il-Liġi, il-Morali, u r-Raġuni* (*Law, Morality, and Reason*, Malta 2008) Professor Mifsud Bonnici simply manages to say all that there is to say. I could not change anything in that book. And I find that all serious thinkers who try to justify any deviation from those ideas are merely engaging in unwarranted hair-splitting or, if they are minor thinkers, blindly following the dominant ideology, to put it as Slavoj Žižek would. During the writing of that book, before Peter Serracino Inglott (1936-2012, a Roman Catholic priest who had been Rector of the University of Malta and Professor of Philosophy) dictated his *Postface* to me at the retirement home for the clergy where he was living at the time, the three of us had dinner together twice, in Valletta, at the British Hotel and at Pippo's Restaurant, during which I sat quietly to listen with intensity to the discussion. When the argument turned to politics – the politics of 2007/08, which have now faded into insignificance, though their consequences are still felt and will be for many long years – I merely listened politely. But when they engaged in hot pursuit of "the truth"

gave me more than one satisfaction. The major one was that the questions dealt with in that book were not only topical but also timely: they have all topped the political agenda of Malta since then. A second satisfaction was the (I believe successful) attempt to portray the indomitable warrior spirit of Professor Mifsud Bonnici's intellect. And there are others.

The definitive impetus for legal history writing came from Giovanni Bonello, one-time judge of that august Strasbourg Court. Dr Bonello is also a historian, having written more than 22 history books. I don't know whether he would want to be called a legal historian, though. Be that as it may, he wrote me an email on 28 March 2012 in which he told me, "I have just finished reading your article on the Criminal Code in *id-Dritt*. It was so refreshing, and challenging, to come across a serious study that debunks, at least in part, the way the neo-colonialists have re-written the past. Our history has often been the victim of frame-ups, and still is. Heartfelt congratulations for the research, the intuitions, the methodology, the discoveries and the conclusions. Glad to see historiography finally moving away from fairy-tale telling. Have not read such compelling history of legislation critique for a long while." This email sealed my desire to write on legal history.

So I would like to thank all of these people for (wittingly or unwittingly) pushing me toward the arduous task of sitting down at the desk, trying to impose some order on a mob of disorderly ideas jumping around like kangaroos, and then type happily away like there's no tomorrow. It is only their merit if I can now collect in one book the legal history essays I wrote between 2011 and 2015.

---

on the beginning of human life, my interest piqued. I agreed hundred per cent with the stance steadfastly taken by Mifsud Bonnici. Despite the admiration I had for Serracino Inglott on other occasions – such as when, a few years earlier during a public talk held in a museum in the ancient Maltese walled city of Mdina, he had expounded upon the meaning of the metaphor of the Centaur – this time I thought that the seasoned philosopher was splitting hairs. Mifsud Bonnici held his (in my eyes more rational) position, out of conviction, not compunction, with resolution and, at times, irascibility. I estimate this episode explains the enigmatic ending of Serracino Inglott's *Postface* to that book. In a world dominated by the utopia of youth (and the reluctance to assume responsibility), Professor Mifsud Bonnici places himself on the opposite side of the fence.

I also would like to thank Kevin Aquilina, Professor and Dean at the Faculty of Laws of the University of Malta, for his attitude. I have not put my finger on it yet, but I know that he transmits a certain positive energy which makes you want to go on and not give up, despite the difficulties.

Thanks are also due to some other friends: Andrea Scagnetti for designing the cover and Sandro Debono of Heritage Malta and Catherine Tabone of the Department of Culture, Malta, for the use of the painting; Maria Pia Arana Barbier for lending a hand with the indices; Joseph Anthony Debono and Walid Nabhan for their invaluable help with the Latin and the Arabic (respectively) when those languages were too obscure for the present writer; Dr Yanika Borg for her help with the essay on the Criminal Code; Dr David A Borg for telling me that since he thinks I'm an eccentric, he therefore feels it's his duty to throw small hints at me every now and then (mostly about arcane books and writings), to enjoy seeing them find their way into my writings; and Dr Antonio Depasquale for his relentless poking fun at my pet subject – he is a beacon of sanity whose ruthless mocking continuously reminds me that history of law is worth-less as an end in itself but could be quite precious if it manages to serve as a tool to understand the contemporary world.

And to one Catherine and one Katrine both Sammut for both telling me the same thing(s) but in completely different languages and ways. I'm usually touched and humbled by their wisdom.

Table of Cases

Table of Authorities

Introduction

THE RELATIONSHIP BETWEEN history and law first appeared as the subject of intellectual reflection in France in the sixteenth century. But this intellectual pursuit grew in importance only with the development of the German historical school of Jurisprudence, a nineteenth-century intellectual movement in the study of German law. The fundamental project of this schoool was the so-called *geschichtliche Rechtswissenschaft*, that is the working out and promotion of a historical science of law. History of Law had to be the queen of all disciplines, the hardcore of the science of law, as it were. For the jurist Friedrich von Savigny (1779–1861), one of the foremost elements of the historical school, only a historical approach could give rise to a truly scientific approach to the law. History was not only the key to understanding, it was also an essential method of the Science of Law.

While still occasionally referring to the development of a science of law (following von Savigny's thoughts expressed in 1815), the French soon adopted an approach which concentrated on historical or geographical particularities, moving them toward history while increasing the distance between them and law. They soon moved toward a positivist history, by focussing on the minutiae of legal documents. One of the consequences of this was that history of law morphed into an auxiliary to history (akin to the history of diplomacy) and into an auxiliary to law (akin to statistics).[1]

There was tension between the historical (or comparative) method, based on observation and induction, and the dogmatic method, based on deduction.

The other major actors in this field were the Italians, who gave academic importance to this field of knowledge, like the French and the Germans, at the end of the nineteenth century.

By that time, legal history had come into contact with a nascent discipline, sociology, particularly the theories of Émile

---

1 HALPÉRIN, J.-L. (2001): "L'histoire du droit constituée en discipline : consécration ou repli identitaire ?" (2001) 4 *Revue d'Histoire des Sciences Humaines* 9, p. 19.

Durkheim's (1858–1917). Two currents developed: one attempted to maintain the contact between legal history and sociology, whereas the other current embraced a backward-looking attitude, favouring the study of mediaeval law, also on account of the traditionalist and monarchist symphathies of many legal historians.

This compartmentalisation seems to have ensued, with positivists who increasingly specialise in technical aspects, legal historians who trade in erudition, and the proponents of other human sciences. In other words, whereas a significant fraction of legal writers originally hoped that history would contribute to the right answer, by removing legislation from the evolution of Law, while attempting an understanding of the Law which would go beyond the text of the Code, the majority of legal history studies retreated to the practing of establishing sources and to erudition.

This has lead to the crucial question, as to who is better equipped to make history of law? The historian, who is not trained in the law? Or the lawyer, who has to inject legal reflections in historical analyses?

Then again, is it legal history or history of law?

What is the subject-matter of history of law? Is it made up of the forms assumed by the law, the concepts, the procedures, the institutions? Or is it made up of the myths, the symbols, the ways in which people see themselves through their rules? Is it phenomena or ideologies? In the final analysis, is it the history of legal ideas or the social history of law?

In certain and different ways, these essays, written over a period of four years (2011-2015), are attempts to answer these questions.

Mark A. Sammut

13 January 2016

Judicial Importation into Maltese Law of Italian Private Law Solutions and Its Implications

This essay first appeared in *Id-Dritt Law Journal*,
published by Għ.S.L., University of Malta, Vol. 25 (2015).

Judicial Importation into Maltese Law of Italian Private Law Solutions and Its Implications

Il diritto è dimensione di una civiltà. Civiltà significa storia, significa un certo contesto storico in tutta la ricchezza delle sue espressioni, ed è peculiare atteggia-mento dello storico [del diritto] quello di collocare il dato che ha di fronte all'interno del contesto che lo ha generato e in cui vive. Egli può e deve ricordare al privatista e al pubblicista, tutti conquistati dai proprii testi normativi, che il testo è sempre rappresentazione d'una realtà retrostante,per giunta rappresentazione parziale e artificiosa.

– Paolo Grossi[1]

Beneath the language of a foreign Law or a foreign legal text there exists a substratum of implied premises and even the words used have connotations, which dictionaries of a particular language might not explain. The legal culture of a country would in many cases have forged concepts and a specialised language which may be different from the prevalent non-legal, 'lay' culture and language of that country. One should be wary of trying to decipher a foreign law or legal document without some introduction into that legal culture.

– Ugo Mifsud Bonnici[2]

Inspiration

THIS ESSAY IS inspired by four paragraphs (10-13) of a Malta Court of Appeal (Civil) judgment of 2009.[3] The appellant argued that there were important differences between the Italian and the

1 GROSSI, P (2007): *Società, Diritto, Stato. Un recupero per il diritto* Giuffrè, Milan, 17. [Law is one of the dimensions of a civilisation. Civilisation means history, a particular historical context in all the richness of its ways of expression. It is the distinguishing attitude of the [legal] historian to place a given fact in the context which gave rise to it and in which it exists. He can and should remind the lawyer who practises private law and the other lawyer who practises public law – both vanquished by the text of their statute books – that a text is always the representation of the reality in the background, an incomplete and forced or studied representation to boot.]

2 MIFSUD BONNICI, U (2004): *An Introduction to Comparative Law* Malta University Press, Malta, 83.

3 *Galea vs Falzon*, Court of Appeal (Civil), 9 October 2009.

Maltese situations being examined by the Court, and that there were also important differences between the relevant provision of the Italian Civil Code and the relevant provision of the Maltese Civil Code.

The Court of Appeal observed that '*għalkemm l-appellant jallega illi hemm differenzi fis-sustanza bejn il-liġijiet Maltin u dawk Taljani, ftit li xejn huwa speċifiku*',[4] ['although the appellant alleges that there are substantial differences between the Maltese and the Italian law, he barely went into the specifics'], and it therefore did not have the opportunity to discuss this possible exception to judicial importation of foreign law through foreign judgments.

In this essay, the present author shall try to discuss the implications of the judicial importation of foreign solutions when the foreign legislation and Maltese legislation do not contain identical provisions.

1. Italian judgments and Italian authors as a source of Maltese law

With varying degrees of controversy, it is generally accepted that the sources of Maltese law are

- the written law,
- customs,
- judicial decisions,
- *negotium juridicum* (or legal transactions),[5]
- equity, and
- authoritative opinions.[6]

4 *Ibid*, para 13.

5 The *Rechtsgeschäft* is 'the means by which legal subjects can change the legal positions of themselves or other persons intentionally. Examples from private law are contracts, terminations of contracts, last wills, transfers of rights, and the creation of rights in rem such as usufruct and mortgage [hypothecs]' – HAGE, J (2009): 'What is a legal transaction?' in DEL MAR, M & BANKOWSKI, Z (EDS.): *Law as Institutional Normative Order* Ashgate, Surrey, 103.

6 GALEA, P: Unpublished lectures on Prolegomena, University of Malta.

For many reasons, which there is no need to enter into here, judicial decisions and authoritative opinions might be both local and foreign.

Let the reader consider the scenario in which a Maltese Civil Court refers to and adopts the reasoning of a foreign judicial decision and foreign authors from the same jurisdiction who seem to confirm the pronouncement in that foreign judicial decision. In the case of Italian judicial decisions, such similarities between judgments and authors are not surprising, even if Italian Courts do not usually disclose their proximity to academia. 'Italian courts,' write Sir Basil Markesinis and Jörg Fedtke, 'are among those which do not cite academic authorities in their judgments, be they of national or international origin.' They point out that 'such citation is prohibited by Art 118.3 of the Rules Concerning the Application of the Code of Civil Procedure (1942).'

But, they continue:

> this does not mean that Italian judges do not consult academic literature. Indeed, there is emerging (and, arguably, widespread) consensus that in the field of private and commercial law some important national innovations have been the result of extra-judicial meetings and exchanges between judges and academics.[7]

In other words, it would seem only natural to find Italian judgments and Italian academics concurring in their opinions, because Italian Courts listen to academics. This traffic of opinions originating from academia and reaching the judiciary is important for the proper understanding of those judgments, since they sometimes end up becoming part of Maltese Civil Law.

2. Implications of judicial importations

When Maltese Courts refer to contemporary Italian judgments, they are therefore indirectly referring to both the evaluation of the

7 MARKESINIS, B & FEDTKE, J (2006): *Judicial Recourse to Foreign Law. A New Source of Inspiration?* Routledge, Oxford 62.

facts and their societal circumstances by the Italian Court, and the doctrinal undercurrents which help to forge the dominant legal culture of the moment in Italy. To put it differently, the Maltese Courts would be obtaining their inspiration from facts taking place in a different society and commented upon by authors trained in a different legal milieu.

This milieu, like every other national milieu, is constantly evolving for many reasons. To highlight only three: (i) legislative interventions by Italy's sovereign power; (ii) changes in society caused by peculiar circumstances obtaining there, some historical, others societal; and (iii) internal developments within the legal community itself. In 2006, Paolo Grossi, highly respected Judge of the Constitutional Court of Italy and academic, expressed this thought in these words: '*È oggi che qualcosa, anzi molto, sta cambiando, e proprio su un piano di* ***psicologia collettiva dei giuristi***'.[8] He then proceeded to explain how the legal community in Italy had been reacting to what it perceived as the strictures of 'exegetic enslavement' (*servitù esegetica*).[9]

Ugo Mifsud Bonnici explains this point elegantly and lucidly:

> Every country has its own legal culture. It is important to distinguish the elements that compose each country's legal culture. The truth is that the law of any given country is not solely that in its statute books or customs, but a whole complex and continuously changing mass of interacting positive laws, ideas and habits.

---

8 GROSSI, *op. cit.*, 15 ['It is today that something, or rather a lot, is changing, and actually on the level of the ***collective psychology of jurists***'] [emphasis added].

9 'Il dato va valutato con attenzione; per buona parte il metodo di lavoro del giurista di oggi è determinato da linee metodologiche che si elaborano lungo il 19° secolo. Il giudizio di mera esegesi, attribuito a questi giuristi, va con tutta probabilità corretto' [The fact has to be evaluated carefully. Much of the work methodology of today's jurist is determined by methodological practices worked out in the 19th century. The consideration that these jurists merely carry out exegesis should most probably be corrected] – FERRANTE, R (2002): *Dans l'ordre établi par le Code civil. La scienza del diritto al tramonto dell'Illuminismo giuridico* Giuffrè, Milan, *passim* and FERRANTE, R (2011): *Codificazione e cultura giuridica* 2nd ed, Giappichelli, Turin, *passim*.

> It is wise for any Court to seek to ascertain the true import of a foreign law not simply through the reading of the text in the original or more so when translated. In Civil Law countries there is more recourse to the quotation of the latest authoritative textbooks. Some study of Comparative Law could acquaint legal practitioners with the basic principles in the understanding of a foreign law.[10]

In Public Law, international developments seem to have a more legitimate place in the judicial importation of foreign concepts and solutions. After all, the liberal democratic modern State is more or less the same all over the West; it places emphasis on the freedoms of the individual and on the market economy.

On the other hand, in Private Law, the implementation of the market economy has taken different national routes. This is one problem which the current European civil law harmonisation project sets out to solve, namely the removal of divergences between national contract law regimes in order to ease cross-border transactions and allow citizens to take full advantage of the internal market, and for which it is also being criticised.[11]

However, the essential point is that the creation of the national Civil Codes in nineteenth-century Europe took place in an ideological context which no longer believed in a European *ius commune* (the law common to all Europeans which had characterised Europe in the High Middle Ages and Early Modernity – the *Ancien Régime* period) but believed wholeheartedly in a shared European legal culture which served as background to the diverse national socio-economic situations.

---

10 MIFSUD BONNICI, U, *op. cit.*, 83-86.

11 HALSON, R & CAMPBELL, D (2013): 'Harmonisation and its discontents: a transaction costs critique of a European contract law' in DEVENNEY, J & KENNY, M (EDS.), *The Transformation of European Private Law Harmonisation, Consolidation, Codification or Chaos?* Cambridge University Press, Cambridge, 100.

3. Not all friends are true: the Italian Civil Code

When contemporary Italian judgments are consulted, it would be wise to avoid the presumption that the Italian and the Maltese Civil Codes always say the same thing. Furthermore, one has to verify which Italian Code one is referring to. Unified Italy has had two Civil Codes, one promulgated in 1865 and the other in 1942.

The 1865 Code followed, more or less, the *Code Napoléon,* that is, the Civil Code of the French of 1804. The lynchpin of Italian Civil Law thus remained property and its ownership, even if the social and historical context of the Italian Code was different from that obtaining in early nineteenth-century France. Because of this orientation, the Civil Code became the legal toolbox of liberal[12] or bourgeois Italy.

The 1942 Code, on the other hand, was heavily influenced by the *Bürgerliches Gesetzbuch* (BGB), the Civil Code of Unified Germany published in 1900[13] and also by German notions which had not made it to the BGB. An example of the latter would be *decadenza* and *prescrizione*. To borrow Barbara Pozzo's words:

> To understand the origin of the differentiation of *decadenza* and *prescrizione* in the Italian [1942] code, unknown to other systems, it is necessary to go back to the mid-nineteenth

---

12 Nineteenth-century liberalism was different from contemporary liberalism (or neo-liberalism, or radical liberalism).

13 "The unification of Germany in 1870 created the political base for the unification of the law. The Pandectists, who dominated the German faculties of law, had the choice of staying on the sidelines or of co-operating. On the grounds that the development of German law was now sufficiently advanced and had achieved completion, many opted in favour of the latter. The *Bürgerliches Gesetzbuch*, introduced in 1900, was accordingly also primarily the work of the Pandectists" – LESAFFER, R (2009): *European Legal History A Cultural and Political Perspective* Cambridge University Press, Cambridge, 471. The Pandectists (an offshoot of Friedrich Carl von Savigny's (1779-1861) historical school) were a German school of thought which believed that, using strict logic, scholars could extrapolate new rules from Justinian's *Corpus juris civilis* and the Pandects, in particular apt at regulating modern socio-economic fact-situations. They opposed codification as they considered rights to exist *de facto* rather than being State-given.

century and the studies which were being pursued into the legal effect of prescription periods and how time runs in legal terms.

The subject was set in a single framework from the conceptual point of view and referred to one single legal regime – that of prescription.

This method of proceeding was accepted by both French and German academic commentators. The notion of prescription embraced several institutes which would be collocated today in quite a different way. Prescription included at one and the same time not only its extinguishing aspect, but also that of acquisition (*usucapione*). The 1865 Italian civil code reproduced this single archetype.

However, after the 1865 civil code had been decreed, Italian academic lawyers came under the influence of their German counterparts, in particular the work of Grawein and Weiss.

German legal thought started to make a distinction between *Präklusivfristen* and so-called *Verjährungsfristen*, but in the German civil code (the BGB), which came into force on 1 January 1900, no specific provisions in the field of *decadenza* were included. However, the code allowed that there were points which legal scholars may have wished to develop.

In contrast to this, the Italian law-makers introduced a differentiation between *decadenza* and *prescrizione* into the 1942 code, a novelty with respect to the 1865 version, following the line of thought coming from German legal scholars which greatly influenced the debate in Italy in the early years of the XXth century.

The outcome of this is that the clear distinction between *decadenza* and *prescrizione*, which is a feature of the legal language of Italian jurists, is non-existent or much more attenuated elsewhere, such as in France, where the expression *délais prefix* is used by legal academics, but not in the code.[14]

---

14 POZZO, B (2006): 'Multilingualism, Legal Terminology and the Problems of Harmonising European Private Law' in POZZO B ET AL. (EDS.): *Multilingualism*

Generally speaking, Malta's Code reproduces most of the provisions of the 1865 Italian Civil Code and, like it, carries two extra topics compared to the *Code Napoléon*: community and possession. The Code's original drafter, Sir Adriano Dingli (1817-1900), 'also consulted the provisions of other leading Continental Codes and the treatises of textwriters of repute. He also referred to the Code of Louisiana, itself based on the *Code Napoléon*.'[15] On account of the needs and mores of the Maltese people, however, on numerous occasions he had to modify the European legislations serving as his model, adding special provisions too.[16] Whereas Harding claims that the Ordinances which later became the Maltese Civil Code were 'more progressive than the *Code Napoléon* because they incorporated provisions containing solutions to the controversies which arose after the promulgation of the *Code Napoléon*',[17] Biagio Andò claims that from the time of the Ordinances, 'the Maltese Code has remained one of the most faithful codes to the original Code Napoleon when compared with the civil codes of other civil law systems which have undergone revision. In fact, the Maltese Code has remained fairly stable.'[18]

In sum, the situation we have at the moment is quadrangular:

On the first side of this quadrangle, we have the 1865 Italian Civil Code, which followed more or less the *Code Napoléon.*

On the second side, the 1942 Italian Civil Code, which was heavily influenced by the provisions of the German Civil Code of 1900 and by notions elaborated by German authors but not incorporated in their country's Civil Code.

---

and the Harmonisation of European Law Kluwer Law International, The Hague, 9 10.

15 HARDING, H W (1994): 'Law' in FRENDO, H & FRIGGIERI, O (EDS.): *Malta Culture and Identity* Ministry for Culture and the Youth, Malta, 216.

16 BILLIET, C (1896): *Lois Civiles de Malte Traduites et annotées et mises en concordance avec le code français, Traduction publiée avec l'autorisation de M. le Premier Président de la Cour d'appel d'Alger,* Collect. de Codes Étrangers XVII, Paris Pedone, Paris, 1.

17 HARDING, *op. cit.*, 216.

18 ANDÒ, B (2011): 'The Role of Judges in Mixed Legal Systems' [2011] *Journal of Civil Law Studies* Vol 4 Issue 2 245.

On the third side, the Maltese Civil Code, which has remained by and large faithful to the original *Code Napoléon*, albeit with interpolations, some of which incorporate autochthonous rules while others reflect rules taken from other codes such as the Code of Louisiana.

On the fourth and last side, the *Code Napoléon* itself, which has undergone numerous amendments over the years.

The quadrangle in the middle is Maltese *praxis*.

The question becomes self-evident. When the Maltese Judge refers to contemporary Italian judgments, can she merely make those decisions hers without first verifying their origins, or at least their legislative bases, to compare them with the Maltese provision(s) at hand? Could there be cases of *faux amis*? Not merely linguistic, but also legal *faux amis* ... false friends which could lead down the wrong path?

Another question raises its head. If the Maltese Judge is going to quote contemporary Italian judgments, why doesn't she, in the light of the above, quote contemporary French judgments as well? There will certainly be cases when a French judgment will be based on a provision the contents of which are closer to our own than the Italian provision dealing with the same subject-matter.

4. The same legislative bases

It is clear that when there is a gap, or *lacuna*, in the law, the Civil Court cannot send the litigants back home on the basis that there is no law which decides their case. If legislation, custom, previous judicial decisions, the volition of the parties themselves, equity, and authoritative opinions are all silent about the facts of the case at hand, and it is not even possible to interpret broadly any of these sources, then it is obvious that the Civil Court has to 'create' a rule 'according to justice and right, and in accordance with the laws and customs of Malta, to the honour of God and the Republic of Malta'.[19] If foreign judgments can offer a solution which fits the

19 This is how the Judge binds herself to carry out her duties when she takes the oath of office – Code of Organisation and Civil Procedure, Chapter 12 of the Laws of Malta, Article 10.

terms of the oath of office,[20] then one cannot see why there should be any obstacle to the judicial importation of it.

The same applies when there is a clear case of ambiguity in Maltese legislation. This might seem an oxymoron, but indeed it is not, for what the present author means here is that it would be preferable if ambiguity were not forced on an otherwise fairly clear provision in order to accommodate an interpretation which is so broad as to almost verge on illegitimacy.

In German legal literature, one finds arguments about the legitimacy of Court creativity in the matter of interpretation. Essentially, the arguments run along the following lines: does the Court, in its interpretation of the statute, respect the 'boundaries of the system and the objectives (teleology) of the statute' or does it not?[21]

The same questions arise with regard to the respect for the boundaries of the system and the teleology of the statute, particularly, when there is no gap in a particular piece of Maltese legislation, which also happens to be unambiguous to boot. In

---

20 Indeed, the oath of office of a judge somehow delimits the functions of the Court by using the old device of concretising an abstract concept by incarnating it in a human being. The abstract functions of the Court become the concrete functions of the Judge. The formula is not just logical, it is beautiful! Unlike the elected Member of Parliament (who represents a part of the electorate and therefore has to be partial), the Judge represents the State and therefore has to be impartial. She is to carry out her functions 'in accordance with the laws and customs of Malta' but within the confines of 'justice and right', and 'to the honour of God', which translates into the Judge's conscience, and to the honour of 'the Republic of Malta', which can only refer to the Sovereignty of the State, namely the boundaries of the administrative and legal setup and the teleology of the law being examined (*vide infra*).

21 German legal literature distinguishes between *Gesetzesimmanente Rechtsfortbildung* and *Gesetzesübersteigende Rechtsfortbildung*, the latter describing the case when Courts exceed the boundaries. LARENZ, K (2008): *Methodenlehre der Rechtswissenschaft* 1st ed., Springer Berlin Heidelberg, Berlin, 366-367. Being unable to read German, the present writer has learnt this through BARKHUYSEN, T, VAN EMMERIK, VL, & UZMAN, J (2010): 'The Dutch Supreme Court: A Reluctant Positive Legislator?' [2010] *Electronic Journal of Comparative Law* Vol 14.3 <http://www.ejcl.org/143/art143-16.pdf> accessed 3 February 2015. If one were to translate the terms used, *Rechtsfortbildung* would mean the 'creation of law by means of case-law', *Gesetzesimmanente* 'that is still covered or implied by positive law', and *Gesetzesübersteigende* 'that goes beyond what is stated by positive law' – the present author would like to thank Dr Werner Miguel Kühn for his assistance.

this case, one doubts whether a Maltese Court is empowered to modernise the law by importing a foreign judgment based on a differently-worded legal provision as this would probably be tantamount to the abrogation of the current law and the enactment of a new law, namely the foreign provision. If the two provisions are not identical, one cannot see how the Maltese Court could adopt the foreign reasoning.

5. Dangers and obstacles in the use of foreign law

There is a chapter[22] in Sir Basil Markesinis and Jörg Fedtke's book, already quoted above, which carries this title. The present author shall not summarise it here, but shall only enumerate the subheadings which add up to a list of dangers and obstacles in the use of foreign law:

- lack of precise information,
- is the information about the foreign legislation and the society which it regulates up-to-date?
- detailed consideration versus generalities ('the use of foreign law is impeded by the fact that it is merely translated into the language of the potential "receiver" rather than packaged in a manner that made it useable by the judges and lawyers of the receiving system'[23]),
- the impact of the socio-economic and political environment,
- legal certainty,
- do courts have enough time to deal with other legal systems?
- the 'depth' of analysis of foreign legal ideas.

22 MARKESINIS, *op. cit.*, 139 *et seq.*

23 *Ibid*, 145.

6. Summing up

Whereas the traditional, nineteenth-century authors, such as Pothier, Pacifici Mazzoni, Giorgi, Ricci, Baudry-Lacantinerie and all the others, be they Italian or French in translation, clearly express ideas which are closer to the spirit and letter of the Maltese Civil Code, contemporary Italian judgments have to be considered with caution, because they might be based on provisions of the 1942 Italian Civil Code which contain rules different from those of its 1865 predecessor and the Maltese Civil Code. It is probably difficult to justify the importation of the reasoning applied to a 1942 provision, the wording of which is different to the Maltese provision on the same subject.

Needless to say, this situation might seem ridiculous - why should twenty-first century Malta still be governed by a nineteenth-century Code? If the time has come to modernise the Code, then Parliament, empowered by the Constitution to make laws, should tackle the matter.

The same degree of care clearly applies in the case of other laws, not just the Civil Code, which the legislator may have copied from Italy or other jurisdictions.

Furthermore, if the foreign provision has remained unchanged, but the legal culture within which it is now being applied has developed significantly, then it follows that contemporary judgments of the country of origin are also suspicious and to be treated as such.

Finally, it would dispel worries of illegitimacy if the importation of the judicial reasoning were justified on the basis of an exercise which evaluates whether the imported foreign reasoning, forged in different administrative and socio-economic conditions, fits in well with the teleology and boundaries of Malta's domestic legal system.

Perhaps, had the appellant in the appeal case mentioned above gone through this exercise, the Court of Appeal would have had the opportunity to make a pronouncement on this point, thereby further clarifying accepted practice.

Historical Facts and Myths surrounding the Criminal Code of Malta

This essay first appeared in *Id-Dritt Law Journal*, published by Għ.S.L., University of Malta, Vol. 22 (2012).

Historical Facts and Myths surrounding the Criminal Code of Malta

Every man calls barbarous
anything which he is not accustomed to.
– Montaigne, *Essais*, I, 31[1]

Diceva Lord Rosebery [...] che Napoli era
la sola città coloniale senza un quartiere europeo;[...]
Napoli può veramente sembrare ad un
viaggiatore che venga dal nord una città coloniale o, se volete,
l'anticipazione d'una città medio-orientale o nordafricana.
– Francesco Compagna (1921-1982),
Italian Minister and intellectual[2]

THE BRITISH OCCUPATION and subsequent *de jure* sovereignty of Malta brought in their wake innovations in Maltese legislation and Law, including the drawing up of a Criminal Code. This Code holds the legal historian's interest because it is indeed a code in the continental sense of the term, but it also contains a conspicuous amount of Common Law procedural principles which, in their country of origin, had until then never been completely codified.[3] Many received 'facts' about the Criminal Code are in fact myths. This essay will examine some of the facts and myths.

1. Mediterranean constitutional workshops

Malta's British connection was not a solitary instance in the Mediterranean. It was indeed the only experiment with a long-

---

1 MONTAIGNE, M (TRS. SCREECH, MA) (2003): *The Complete Essays* Penguin, London, 231.

2 *Debates*, Italian Chamber of Deputies, 24 October 1969. [Lord Rosebery used to say [...] that Naples was the only colonial city not to have a European quarter; [...] To a traveller coming from the North, Naples may really look like a colonial city or, if you prefer, the foretaste of a Middle Eastern or North African city] Lord Rosebery (1847-1929), a Liberal Imperialist, was Prime Minister of Great Britain from 5 March 1894 till 22 June 1895.

3 In most instances neither have they been ever since. – DEZZA, E (2003): '... Felicemente disposano le tradizioni della scuola italiana alle libertà inglesi' in VINCIGUERRA, S. (ED.), *Leggi Criminali per l'Isola di Malta e Sue Dipendenze (1854)* CEDAM, Padua, CCCXVII.

term successful outcome, but Britain had already tried to gain a foothold elsewhere in the central Mediterranean.[4] After a bird's-eye view of these other instances, we shall zero in on the Maltese situation.

1.1 The Anglo-Corsican Kingdom[5]

Corsica requested British protection upon formal secession from France in 1794.[6] The ensuing short-lived Anglo-Corsican Kingdom's Constitution[7] stated that nobody could be deprived of his freedom or property if not upon a lawful decision of the recognized tribunals,[8] detainees should be brought before the competent Tribunal within twenty-four hours to have their case lawfully adjudged,[9] and if the detention were declared vexatious, the detainee was entitled to compensation.[10]

1.2 The Sicilian Constitution[11]

When the French invaded, the King of Naples was forced to move his Court to Palermo, where he was reduced to a state of

4 Indeed, we shall consider Cyprus, Minorca, and Gibraltar as outside our purview.

5 1794-1796. This Kingdom was characterized by internal political confusion. – SERPENTINI, A L (ED.) (2006): *Dictionnaire Historique de la Corse* Albiana, Ajaccio, France, 869.

6 SERPENTINI, *op. cit.*, 730-737.

7 Decreed in 1794. The Constitution stated that the 'free and independent' (Preamble) People of Corsica recognized that legislative (Title I, Articles 2 and 3) and executive (Title V, Articles 1, 2, and 3) powers belonged to the King of Great Britain. At first blush, this Constitution would seem a simple codification of the English constitution, but in reality it also encompassed principles from the French Constitution of 1791 and traditional Corsican institutions. British parliamentarism and habeas corpus were combined with monocameralism, while official recognition of Catholicism as the people's religion with Lockeian tolerance; some articles were literal translations of the 1791 French Constitution and one finds the 1755 Consiglio di Stato and the ancient pievi. – SERPENTINI, *op. cit.*, 282.

8 Article 1 of Title VIII, "Of Individual Freedom and Freedom of the Press".

9 Article 2.

10 Article 3.

11 1810-1815.

'continuing colonial status' and dependence on British military protection.[12]

The 1812 Palermitan Constitution is probably the most significant product of the 'constitutional engineering workshops'[13] ignited by the British presence in the Mediterranean.[14] § 35, Chapter I, Title III provided for the *habeas corpus* principle, whereas Chapter XXX for trial by jury.

Between 1810 and 1815, but mostly in the last two years of that quinquennium, discussions on the failed codification process fuelled Sicilian politics, particularly because codes were deemed implements for the Constitution's principles.[15] Though surely succumbing to the contagion of the 'Anglomania'[16] infecting Sicily,[17] the Maltese were also probably alive to opinions that the 1812

---

12 DAVIS, JA (2006): *Naples and Napoleon. Southern Italy and the European Revolutions, 1780-1860* Oxford University Press, Oxford, 289.

13 ['*Laboratori di ingegneria costituzionale*'] It is noteworthy, as an aside, to highlight along with Italian authors, the Constitution's contradiction stemming from the coexistence in the instrument of a French mentality which views codes as an extension of the Constitution and repeated references to the English constitutional model. *Vide* NOVARESE, D (2002): 'Fra Common Law e Civil Law. Il Jury nell'Esperienza Costituzionale Siciliana 1810-1815)' in *Historia Constitucional. Revista electrónica*, No. 3, June 2002, Spain http//www.seminariomartinezmarina.com/ojs/index.php/historiaconstitucional/article/viewFile/177/157, accessed 11 August 2011 paragraph 21.

14 This phenomenon ultimately led to constitutional projects which served as alternatives to the French templates spread first by the Jacobins and later by French conquests and the Napoleonic models they brought in their wake. – NOVARESE, *op. cit.*, paragraph 2.

15 *Ibid.*, paragraph 33. 'The Sicilian Constitution of 1812 has won some notoriety as that "which for the first time laid down in writing the glorious principles of the unwritten constitution of Britain" (Webster, i, 82). But this deliberate copy of an elusive foreign model came about partly through a chapter of accidents: Bentinck [Britain's Minister in Sicily], far from imposing it, deplored it before he came to acquiesce in it.' – ROSSELLI, J (1956): *Lord William Bentinck & the British Occupation of Sicily 1811-1814* Cambridge University Press, Cambridge, 44.

16 ROSSELLI, J (1974): *Lord William Bentick the making of a liberal imperialist* Sussex University Press, Edinburgh, 157.

17 All this must have also contributed to the Maltese determination voluntarily 'to place their Island home under the protection of Great Britain and to recognize the King of that country as their sovereign.' – CREMONA, JJ (1994): *The Maltese Constitution and Constitutional History Since 1813* Publishers Enterprises Group, San Ġwann, Malta, 1. On the other hand, the self-same Cremona (CREMONA,

Sicilian Constitution was a 'monstrous melange of English veneer and French corruption':[18]

> *[i] modelli costituzionali d'Inghilterra, espressamente richiamati anche se in realtà recepiti solo in misura parziale, e non senza la mediazione delle idee dei* philosophes *e del modello adottato dai costituenti francesi.*[19]

The Maltese reception was more or less identical.[20]

1.3 The United States of the Ionian Islands[21]

Promulgated in 1841, the Ionian Islands' Criminal Code took 25 years to draft, explaining that 'high level of perfection'[22] which

---

JJ (1990): *Selected Papers 1946-1989* (Publishers Enterprises Group, Marsa, Malta, 78) speculates about 'an element of reaction' among the British to 'the utter failure of Bentinck's "English Constitution" in Sicily'.

18 NOVARESE, D: 'Tra Francia e Inghilterra. Riflessioni siciliane sulla carta del 1812' in ROMANO, A (ED.) (1998): *Il Modello Costituzionale Inglese e la sua Recezione nell'Area mediterranea tra la Fine del '700 e la prima Metà dell' '800* Giuffrè editore, Milan, 804, quoting the Abate Tognini.

19 PADOA-SCHIOPPA, A (2003): 'La Giuria Penale a Malta 1811-1854)' in VINCIGUERRA: *Leggi Criminali per l'Isola di Malta e Sue Dipendenze (1854)* CEDAM, Padua, CCCLII. [the English constitutional models, expressly invoked but in reality only partially received, and not without the mediation of the ideas of the philosophes and the model adopted by the French constituents].

20 There were three ways in which the Sicilian constitution could be seen: 'as the outcome of deliberate British policy; as the hobby-horse of a Whiggish proconsul; or as the spontaneous achievement of the Sicilian people, with which Britain and her Minister had nothing to do' and the British "propaganda machine" had only to chose which narrative to promote and exploit. – ROSSELLI, *op. cit.* 1956, 65. This analysis could give us a new perspective on law-making in British Malta.

21 1815-1864. The Ionian Islands (Corfu, Cephalonia, Zante, Lefkas, Ithaca, Cerigo, Paxos) belonged to Venice from the 15th century up till 1797 when France conquered Venice. Then they made up the Republic of the Seven Islands from 1800 to 1807 when they were ceded again to France. They became a British protectorate in 1815.

22 VINCIGUERRA, S (2008): 'Umanità delle Pene Detentive, Prevenzione del Reato e Ristoro del Danno' in VINCIGUERRA, S (ED.): *Codice Penale degli Stati Uniti delle Isole Jonie (1841)* CEDAM, Padua, IX. [*un alto grado di perfezione*].

gained the favour of no less than Carrara himself.[23] It owes its significant historical value to the mishmash of traditions which forged it: legal (Venetian law,[24] Romano-Canonical *ius commune*, codified natural law, Common Law, local customary law) and linguistic (Italian, Hellenic, English).[25]

The Maltese found it attractive because it followed the 1807 Code of Napoleonic Italy mediated by the 1819 Code of the Two Sicilies.[26] At the same time, it received at least four typical Common Law principles: the hearsay rule, the opinion rule, the privilege against self-incrimination and the guilty plea.[27]

With these historically relevant antecedents in mind, we can now succinctly relate the Maltese Criminal Code's genesis, and then analyse some of the myths which surround it.

2. Chronology of the 1854 Criminal Code's genesis

Like neighbouring territories, Malta began experiencing the British expansionist policy of creating a 'chain of stations useful [to Britain] both in war and in commerce',[28] a by-product of which was the production of new legislation, including a new Criminal

23 COLAO, F (2008): 'Carrara e alcuni «Delitti di Pericolo Comune» del Codice Jonio' in VINCIGUERRA: *Codice Penale degli Stati Uniti delle Isole Jonie (1841)* CEDAM, Padua, CLXIV. [*grandissima simpatia*].

24 A "heretical" version of the Romano-Germanic tradition.

25 DEZZA, E (2008): 'Istituti di Common Law nel Codice di Procedura Penale Jonio' in VINCIGUERRA: *Codice Penale degli Stati Uniti delle Isole Jonie (1841)* CEDAM, Padua, CLXXI.

26 *Ibid.*, CLXXII. At first the Maltese Commission wanted to work on the Ionian Islands Code, but then discarded it in favour of the Neapolitan Code. JAMESON, A (1844): *Report on the Proposed Code of Criminal Laws for the Island of Malta and its Dependencies* Government Press, Malta, 3. The Commission's decision seems rational: why work on a derived Code when you can work directly on the original?

27 *Ibid.*, CLXXIII.

28 To use Prime Minister Grenville's words, quoted by ROSSELLI, *op. cit.* 1974, 116.

Code.[29] It is logical to proceed with a quick synthesis[30] of the timeline of the Code's drawn-out gestation and parturition.

i. In 1831, a Commission is appointed, charged with the drafting of five codes, including a Criminal Code. Its members: Judge Ignazio Gavino Bonavita and four others: one Maltese and three British.[31]

ii. The Commission very soon splits into two fronts: the Maltese insist on a Code inspired by the Ionian Islands' or the Two Sicilies'; the British are intent on a Code inspired by Common Law principles. The Secretary of State for the Colonies intervenes, siding with the Maltese.

iii. A new Commission[32] is appointed in 1834, after the first one is dissolved.

---

29 In a few telling passages, Jameson (*op. cit.*) writes that 'the Code was to regulate the natives of Malta, who had for forty years been accustomed to the mild administration of British Governors and the enlightened spirit of our Colonial administration; and were now privileged with many free institutions of British origin, unknown in the Kingdom of Naples'. He then goes on, quite bluntly, 'The new Code, moreover was destined to affect a large number of native Englishmen, resident in or resorting to the Island, which besides being the station of a considerable garrison and the wintering quarters of the Mediterranean Fleet, is the resort of many travellers and invalids, and the central point of the steam communication of the Mediterranean and of our communication with India' (p. 4). Further on, he repeats that 'native British subjects, and it may be a numerous portion of them are made amenable of these Criminal Laws, and may become subject to periods of imprisonment which would be altogether revolting to the public opinion of the British people' (p. 24). Even at the end of his long report, he writes that 'the less objectionable the project can be rendered, before it be [put into operation], it is the more likely to meet with the confidence of the Maltese, as well as of the British Residents in Malta' (p. 146).

30 Based on the accounts given by Dr Albert Ganado (1949-50) in 'The Historical Development of the Criminal Code' in *Law Journal*, Nos. 4, 5, and 6 (University Student's Law Society, Valletta) and Judge Paolo De Bono (1897) in his *Sommario della Storia della Legislazione in Malta* (Tipografia del Malta, Valletta) 279–328.

31 Namely Claudio Vincenzo Bonnici, Chief Justice John Stoddart, Barron Field (First Judge of the Supreme Court of Gibraltar) and John Kirkpatrick (Chief Justice of the Ionian Islands). Field and Kirkpatrick are replaced by Attorney-General Robert Langslow in 1832.

32 It was composed of Bonavita and Bonnici and three other Maltese jurists, judges Giuseppe Francesco Falzon and Francesco Chapelle, and lawyer Filippo Torreggiani.

The following year, it submits a Draft Criminal Code and a Draft Criminal Procedure Code.

iv. Nothing comes out of these efforts because of heated arguments and a policy of delay embraced by the British administration.

v. From 1839 to 1842, Bonavita, Falzon and Chapelle re-examine the two Codes and amalgamate them. The 1842 project is then evaluated by Scottish lawyer Andrew Jameson[33] whose report is published in 1844.

vi. The Draft is further amended and published again in 1848, following Jameson's re-evaluation, Adriano Dingli's analysis, Antonio Micallef's revision and the Council of Government's debates.

vii. The 1848 draft, printed again in 1850, is once more examined by the Maltese Council of Government, and directly amended by the Legislative Council in London as regards crimes against religion (1852-1853).

viii. In January 1854, London finally and definitively approves the Code which the Governor promulgates the following March.

3. Common Law *versus* Continental Law myth

Not too long ago, a widely-held view was eloquently and elegantly rehashed thus:

> in Malta, we wisely and conveniently adopted continental law for substance but remained shrewd enough to adopt the libertarian norms and canons of British Common Law for criminal procedure, thereby adopting the accusatorial rather than the inquisitorial system and introducing trial by jury as early as 1815.[34]

33 1811-1870.

34 BORG, T (2010): 'Malta, France and UK: Legacy in History' in *The Times* (Allied Newspapers, Valletta 4 December 2010) 8.

This statement invites us to amplify and qualify it from a historical point of view, particularly since its proposition is predicated on the notions that (i) the Common Law's membrane is impermeable to the civil-law extracellular environment around it; (ii) the Maltese wanted the Anglo-Saxon jury system; and (iii) the Common Law was/is more liberal than Continental Law.

3.1 *Accusatorial* procedure?

Despite one's preconceptions, continental codes of the first half of the 19th century *did* contemplate a dialectical debate similar to the Common Law model. This allowed the Maltese legislator to cull rules from the Neapolitan Code, fitting them easily in the Anglo-Saxon matrix.[35] Of equal importance is the fact that among Jameson's amendments only those which were completely incompatible with Italian penal traditions were rejected by Maltese jurists.[36]

It is undeniable that – as Heidelberg's Professor Mittermaier remarked in 1854 – Malta's criminal procedure law is based on the Common Law principles of full public transparency, equal conditions for defence and prosecution, and full freedom to conduct a close examination of the evidence, but it is equally undeniable that the new procedural structure retained part of the genetic heritage of, on the one hand, the ancient Compilations of the Order of St. John and the 1784 Municipal Code and, on the other, the legal tradition of the Continent, especially Naples.[37]

---

35 DEZZA, *op. cit.* 2003, CCCXXVI. E.g., the rules on i. exceptions of nullity and incompetence; ii. accused appearing unfettered; iii. deaf-mutes; iv. useless protractions by advocates; v. judges' ability to intervene with flickering and unruly witnesses; vi. publicity of sittings (and the exception of in camera proceedings); etc. On the other hand, when the Maltese compilers of the Code borrowed a provision from the Law of England (on "barratry" – abuses by advocates and legal procurators) which did not exist in either the French or Neapolitan Code, Jameson criticized them for choosing a provision that had fallen into 'deserved desuetude' and proposed to leave it out. – JAMESON, A, *op. cit.*, 63.

36 CADOPPI, *op. cit.*, XCIV. The two most prominent jurists to take these positions were Antonio Micallef and Adriano Dingli.

37 LUPARIA, L & GARBAGNATI, G (2003): 'Il Processo Penale Maltese tra Modello Adversary e Radici Continentali' in VINCIGUERRA: *Leggi Criminali per l'Isola di Malta e Sue Dipendenze (1854)* CEDAM, Padua, CCCXXXIX. Mittermaier

An analysis of the 1854 procedural laws demonstrates that the "accusatorial" tag with which Maltese criminal procedure has been labelled is only partially supported by the characteristics of some of its fundamental principles.[38]

In the Code's structure of trial by jury, the quintessential adversary system principles of orality, cross-examination, publicity, immediacy and continuous concentration are made to coexist with continental rules on witnesses' examination and the intervention by the presiding judge.[39]

Let us consider four of these elements in quick succession:

i. Whereas in traditional Common Law systems the re-direct examination at the end of the cross-examination is carried out by the parties themselves, a post-1854 amendment to the Maltese Criminal Code re-introduced the '*impinguazione delle prove*'[40] rule giving the Court the right[41] to ask questions additional to those already posed by prosecution and defence.[42] The 1784 Municipal Code had recognized this Romano-Canonical, inquisitorial-process right, since it had long been adhered to in Malta.[43]

ii. The 1854 Code laid down that the inquiring magistrate draws up a *procès verbal* which has probatory force without, however, there being any cross-examination during the inquiry.[44] It is true that nothing could impede the subsequent *viva voce*

was of the opinion that the Maltese Code was better than the *code pénal* because it had found how to '*bene apprezzare i progressi della scienza e della legislazione italiana, non trascurando di far uso delle leggi criminali d'Inghilterra, ed esaminando bene le domande della scienza e della giustizia, egualmente che i bisogni della società*' [appreciate properly the progress registered in Italian legal knowledge and legislation, without overlooking English criminal laws, while evaluating in an appropriate fashion the needs of legal science and justice, as well as those of society] – COLAO, *op. cit.*, CXXXV.

38 *Ibid.*, CCCXLIX.

39 *Ibid.*, CCCXL.

40 Literally meaning "fattening of the evidence", this collocation belongs to Neapolitan juridical terminology.

41 Originating in Neapolitan law.

42 Art. 433 of the 1900 edition.

43 Libro Secondo, Capo Primo, § XXV. – LUPARIA L ET AL., *op. cit.*, CCCXLII.

44 Art. 464.

examination of persons mentioned in the *procès verbal*, but there is an inversion of the rule (oral cross-examination) and the exception (written evidence *ante iudicem*), denoting a departure from the classical rules obtaining in the courts of the then British Empire.[45]

iii. A guilty plea did not remove the Court's power – inspired by the *Ancien Régime* vision of the judge as *dominus* of the search for the truth, and thus unrestrained by the will of the parties – to order that the case be continued as if the accused had not declared himself guilty.[46]

iv. The *ex officio* obligatory nature of the criminal action is another inquisitorial, not Common Law (accusatorial), principle.[47]

3.2 Trial by *which* jury?

It is true that in 1810, the Maltese agent in London demanded that trial by jury be established,[48] but did the Maltese have in mind the *Anglo-Saxon* trial by jury?

According to J.J. Cremona, 'in Malta trial by jury was [...] introduced gradually and to some extent also grudgingly. [... I]t was the Maltese themselves who [...] petitioned [...] for the introduction of the jury system'.[49] We shall not argue that the Maltese were keen on trial by jury because they doubted the Judiciary's integrity,[50] but that the 1811 petition requested the introduction of

45 LUPARIA ET AL., *op. cit.*, CCCXLV.

46 *Ibid.*, CCCXLVII. For the situation obtaining at the time of writing, the reader is referred to article 392A (enacted by Act III/2002).

47 DEZZA, *op. cit.* 2003, CCCXXII. The Maltese provisions were taken verbatim from the 1819 Neapolitan Code, itself inspired by the 1807 Code of Napoleonic Italy.

48 GANADO, A (2003): 'La Storia del Codice Penale di Malta del 1854. Un breve ragguaglio' in VINCIGUERRA: *Leggi Criminali per l'Isola di Malta e Sue Dipendenze (1854)* CEDAM, Padua, XXX.

49 CREMONA, *op. cit.* 1990, 86-87.

50 Perhaps the Maltese embraced the jury system not so much because they despised the inquisitorial system, but for the reasons underlying the Avviso of 14 June 1805. This Avviso 'recounts that Aloisia Caruana was imprisoned for having attempted to bribe the Penal Judge of the Grand Court of Valletta, with an ounce of Sicilian gold, in order to ensure a favourable outcome in her appeal. It seems

trial by jury '*o nel modo proprio del diritto inglese, o secondo i nostri usi antichi, che prevedevano la possibilità di ricorrere in appello al Consiglio popolare avverso le sentenze dei giudici*'.[51] So, the term "jury" in reality concealed two absolutely different systems, as the English trial by jury had almost nothing in common with the model whereby on appeal justice is entrusted to a political entity such as the *Consiglio popolare*.[52]

3.3 As early as *1815*?

The early trial by jury was a 'limited' and 'modified' version.[53]

Trial by jury *was* introduced in 1815, but its scope was limited to the Court of Piracy. 'The system adopted was the traditional English system of a Grand Jury and a Petty Jury, and the verdicts of jurors (twelve in number as in England) had to be unanimous.'[54] In 1829, then, 'a "modified" form of trial by jury was legislatively introduced in respect of the gravest crimes'.[55]

Writing as late as 1843, Jameson observes that 'the right of trial by Jury [being] limited [...] to a few rare cases [was] one of the principal causes, that the institution in Malta has not been attended

---

that she had already been convicted of a criminal offence; and the judge whom she attempted to bribe, one Doctor Vincenzo Caruana Zerafa, had been listed to hear her appeal. [...] This Avviso had a wider significance because it was issued in the weeks following the anti-Semitic disturbances during which the Administration had interfered in the judicial process to exact a higher sentence for convicted offenders. [...] This interference had caused significant alarm in Malta. It became one of many complaints about Ball's administration that was recounted in a Petition to the Crown.' – HOUGH, B & DAVIS, H (2010): *Coleridge's Law. A Study of Coleridge in Malta* Open Book Publishers, Cambridge, 241. In other words, the Maltese might have looked at the jury system to assuage their fears that members of the judiciary might kowtow to the will of one of the parties, or even worse, to the will of the Executive, tempted by a bribe or a promotion.

51 [either according to the English law model, or else according to our ancient usages, which contemplated the possibility of lodging an appeal with the Consiglio popolare against the sentences meted out by judges] *Vide* GANADO, *op. cit.* 1949-50, *passim*, for more details.

52 PADOA-SCHIOPPA, *op. cit.*, CCCLIII.

53 JAMESON, *op. cit.*, 141.

54 CREMONA, *op. cit.* 1990, 87.

55 *Idem.*

with all the advantages which might have been expected from it.'[56]

3.4 The British *liberal* spirit?

It has been mythified that the British liberal spirit infiltrated the Maltese legal system.[57] Considered with particular reference to

---

56 JAMESON, *op. cit.*, 142. Jameson enumerates some of these advantages: 'the diffusion of general information and a particular acquaintance with the practical operation of the Laws'; 'creating an attachment to the principles on which they are founded; and the promotion of individual happiness and elevation of character by the frequent exercise of these important duties' (p. 142). The "Young Maltese Advocate" (ANON. (1870): *Annotazioni alle Leggi Criminali per l'Isola di Malta e Sue Dipendenze da Servire di Guida al Giurato per cura d'un giovane Avvocato maltese*, Tipo-Litografia Anglo-Maltese, Valletta) recalls that '*i Commissionari di Sua Maestà per la formazione di nuovi codici di legge, nel loro rapporto fatto al Governo il dì 30 settembre 1835 dicevano in termini espressi, che era certo che il Giurì come stabilito in Inghilterra non era praticabile in Malta, e che come vi è stato introdotto e regolato, credevano essere generale opinione che non avesse sortito l'effetto propostosi nella sua istituzione*' [in their report to the Government of the 30 September 1835, Her Majesty's Commissioners appointed to compile the new law codes, expressly said that trial by jury as obtained in England was not practicable in Malta, and that they considered it the general opinion that the way it was introduced and regulated in Malta would not have brought about the effects proposed by its establishment] (p. 8). This writer was writing protected by anonymity in 1870, whole decades after the introduction of trial by jury, and he sat on the fence, '*senza entrare nell'esame della questione se sia stata corretta la detta asserzione*' [without analysing whether the said assertion had been correct]. Might one have reasonably expected a defence of trial by jury? What are we to infer from the lack of such a defence? One hundred and forty-one years later, the Editor of *The Sunday Times* received a letter (SAMMUT, F (no relation to the present author) (2011): 'Reluctant to serve as jurors' (Allied Newspapers, Valletta 9 October 2011) 18) which might hold a clue: 'On September 25, columnist Michela Spiteri wrote: "I've always failed to comprehend the great lengths people will go through to run away from jury duty". The answer is quite simple. People hate it, and for good reason. Apart from all the hassle that those chosen for jury duty have to go through, they often have to see to problems at home, cannot afford to lose income or take time off from work, whether they are employed or have their own business, and are reluctant to give up quality time with their family. Some trials by jury can last weeks on end, and this could disrupt jurors' life considerably. Besides, those chosen to serve as jurors are not paid since this is considered to be an obligation to do one's duty towards one's country. And one must also mention the pressure that builds up on jurors in the course of the trial'.

57 LUPARIA, *op. cit.*, CCCXXXVIII, quoting WH Harding. It would seem that this idea of the liberal spirit began with Sir Hector Grieg, Superintendent of Quarantine and Chief Secretary to Governor Henry Bouverie (1836-1843). In his letter to Andrew Jameson of 2 August 1842 he writes, 'I have received a letter from Mr Under Secretary Hope intimating to me, that Lord Stanley has approved of the

the Criminal Code, this statement strictly speaking refers to the law of procedure. But over time it has been inflated, and there now seems to be a myth that the British *liberal* spirit permeated even the substantive law.

One has to ask: what *liberal* spirit? To justify the myth's perpetuation, it has to pass a double litmus test: was the Common Law liberal by the standards of *those* times *and* is it liberal by *today's* standards?

Let us consider four examples.

1. The only explicit objections raised to capital punishment were Monsignor Leopoldo Fiteni's and Adriano Dingli's,[58] unless, of course, the death sentence is considered a manifestation of liberalism.[59] Indeed, the Maltese members of the Commission

---

recommendation of Governor [...] Bouverie, that you should be employed in revising and reporting on the projected Criminal Code of Malta, as drawn up by the Maltese Commissioners, with the view of infusing into the Code (which is taken from the Neapolitan Code) the more liberal and enlightened spirit of English Criminal Law' – quoted by Jameson himself (JAMESON, *op. cit.*, 2).

58 During the 1850 Council of Government debates. – GANADO, *op. cit.* 2003, XXXIX, CADOPPI, *op. cit.*, CXIV.

59 It has been opined that since de Rohan's Municipal Code envisaged the death penalty for thirteen crimes, it was 'one of the most barbarous in existence' (LEE, HI (1964): 'British Policy towards the Religion, ancient Laws and Customs in Malta 1824-1851' in *Melita Historica*, 4(1964)1, http//www.judiciarymalta.gov.mt/file.aspx?f=442 accessed 20 August 2011,1). Yet, if we can rely on the testimony of one single, albeit renowned visitor during the last years of Grand Master Pinto's reign, 'The police indeed is much better regulated than in the neighbouring countries, and assassinations and robberies are very uncommon; the last of which crimes the grand master punishes with the utmost severity. But he is said, perhaps in compliance with the prejudice of his nation, to be much more relax [sic] with regard to the first' – BRYDONE, P (1773): *A Tour through Sicily and Malta in a Series of Letters to William Beckford, Esq. of Somerly in Suffolk.* Vol. I W. Strahan and T. Cadell, London, 331. (Brydone was a Freemason (BRYDONE, *ibid.*, Vol. II (1774) 45), and it would seem the tour he embarked on was a typical Masonic tour.) Earlier on, the same author relays what he must have heard about the punishments meted out to the slaves who revolted in 1749: 'The suspected persons were instantly seized and put to the torture, and soon confessed the whole plot. The executions were very terrible. One hundred and twenty-five were put to death by various torments. Some were burned alive, some were broken on the wheel, and some were torn to pieces by the four galleys rowing different ways, and each bringing off its limb.' This probably makes it clear why the law was so severe but its application relaxed: it gave the Grand Master elbow-space within which to exercise his discretion. Being politically savvy, (probably) an

were instructed by the British authorities that the death penalty was *not* to be abolished.[60]

Strongly in favour of the death penalty, Jameson argued against the doctrine of punishment reduction when attenuating circumstances subsisted, as its 'practical effect,' he wrote, 'would be the tacit abolition of capital punishment in all cases.'[61]

It was Cesare Beccaria[62] who put forth the first argument ever against the death penalty[63] and an Italian Code the first ever to abolish it.[64] The Italian (Catholic) tradition, to which Malta belonged, favoured a humane approach, based on clemency, forgiveness and pity – as opposed to the "vindictive" or retributive tendencies of the Anglo-Saxon tradition.[65]

2. As regards sexual mores, Jameson was adamant

enlightened autocrat, and a member of a monastic order, no Grand Master in his right senses would have abused of his discretion if he wanted to eschew a popular insurgence. The Knights must have been aware of the folklore which kept alive the memory of the 1428 uprising against Gonsalvo Monroy, and of the 1282 Sicilian Vespers. Were all Ancien Régime rulers some sort of King John of Victorian and twentieth-century Robin Hood romances?

60 GANADO, *op. cit.* 2003, XXXVI. Even though it must be said that in his Report, Jameson at least expressed the view that 'this punishment ought to be confined nominally as well as actually to the highest order of crimes' – JAMESON, *op. cit.*, 15.

61 JAMESON, *op. cit.*, 52.

62 † 1794. Jameson calls Bentham one 'of the most liberal writers upon the subject of criminal Law' (*op. cit.*, 85). Since Bentham assimilated much of Beccaria's thought, it is reasonable to deduce that Jameson considered Beccaria too a liberal.

63 Beccaria was in favour of long, even painful periods of detention. Jameson refers to this explicitly and finds in it 'strange inconsistency'. He derides the underlying notion that 'it is not the intensity of the punishment but its extension which produces the greater effect upon the human mind'. And so, for these reasons, he is all out in favour of the death penalty. – JAMESON, *op. cit.*, 12-13.

64 The Tuscan Code (or Leopoldino) of 1786.

65 CADOPPI, *op. cit.*, CXIV. The Italian tendency would seem ready to sacrifice "just desert" in the name of humaneness. If we go back to the fourteenth century, we find that Neapolitan Post-Glossator Lucas de Penna said, '*Accusator, qui ad accusationem non invidiae livore, sed justitiae zelo procedit, salutis publicae custodiam gerit*', paraphrased as 'accusations against criminals […] should be preferred, not in

the Maltese Code should criminalise incest,[66] an idea strongly resisted by the Maltese jurists. He also argued in favour of an increased punishment for the "unnatural offence" (that is, bestiality).[67] Jameson's position was consonant with the Common Law's Puritan ethos, which hinders the extrication of law from morality.[68]

Following the emancipation from *Ancien Régime* prudishness, the penal Codes of Italy, France and other juris-

---

a spirit of vengeance or of hatred, but in one of justice' – ULLMAN, W (1946): *The Medieval Idea of Law as Represented by Lucas de Penna* Methuen & Co. Ltd., London, 160.

66 JAMESON, *op. cit.*, 84, 113. Jameson seems unable to transcend his own culture, which he perceives as setting the standard as if it were a behaviour Greenwich Mean Time of sorts. 'I have been unable,' he writes, 'to discover the reasons which have induced the learned Persons who framed the Code Pénal of France to omit all prohibition of this offence. The mere infrequency of its occurrence in Malta is no good reason why such a revolting offence against social morals and the purity of domestic life should pass unpunished, when it does occur' (p. 84). It is true that he argues that 'Filangieri and Bentham, two of the most liberal writers upon the subject of criminal Law allow the propriety, of a penal provision on this subject, as essential to domestic purity and the encouragement of marriage' (p. 85). Interestingly, the Maltese were more liberal by today's standards on this matter.

67 JAMESON, *op. cit.*, 112. 'It appears inconsistent with the moral distinctions which are plain to every mind,' he writes, 'to punish this offence with twenty five months to three years imprisonment and at the same time to award the punishment of four to six years' imprisonment for bigamy, and thirteen to fifteen years for the offence of stealing the Eucharist.' And then the racist in him raises its ugly head: 'Such a scale of punishment is not apt to improve the public notions with regard to the criminality of these respective offences, and no man who is acquainted with the South of Europe will hesitate to declare, that the tone of public sentiment with regard to the offences implied in the Article in question is much in need of improvement' (pp. 112-113). What is he saying exactly? That the Maltese at large were tolerant of unusual but harmless people who obtain sexual gratification from animals? What is particularly wrong with not wanting to punish deviant sexual behaviour? A liberal mind would argue for other reactions to such behaviour, but certainly not imprisonment....

68 It is only recently that a liberal understanding has appeared thanks to Hart and Feinberg, which insists that a criminal offence implies the unlawful production of a harm caused to others. But despite these appeals, Anglo-American law is even today reluctant in separating sexual morality from the law.

dictions assumed a tolerant attitude toward "irregular" sexual behaviour, such as incest, bestiality, and homosexuality.[69]

3. Though aware of 'objections justly made to it', Jameson is saddened that the

> punishment of Whipping [had] been rejected. [...I]t might be retained in cases of juvenile depravity [...] It [was] retained in the Law of England [...] and [had been recently] adopted by universal consent of Parliament and of the Country [...] A query was accordingly addressed [...] to the Code Commissioners and Crown Advocate suggesting the propriety of retaining the punishment for such Cases. But it was answered that the public feeling of Malta was inimical to this punishment which was considered as the most atrocious of punishments not capital.[70]

4. With regard to theft, it was another Italian, Gaetano Filangieri,[71] who castigated the "liberal" English for the severity of their laws. Had the English "liberal" spirit been applied, the punishment for theft under Maltese law would *not* have been, by the standards of those times, mild.

During the 1850 debates, reference was made to English law on theft and to its punishments so harsh as to induce witnesses not to appear when summoned, jurymen to refuse finding guilt, and judges to seek ways and means how not to convict.[72]

4. Scots Law

Is there any connection between Maltese and Scots Criminal Law?

---

69 CADOPPI, *op. cit.*, CXVI.

70 JAMESON, *op. cit.*, 18.

71 † 1788. Filangieri too is (rightly) considered by Jameson a liberal (*op. cit.*, 85).

72 DI RENZO VILLATA, M G (2003): "Da Filangieri a Malta: Il Caso del Furto" in VINCIGUERRA (ED.), *Leggi Criminali per l'Isola di Malta e Sue Dipendenze (1854)* CEDAM, Padua, CCLXXXII.

4.1 Andrew Jameson

Jameson proposed amendments to two-thirds of the Draft Code's provisions, concentrating on the substantive part.[73] Why was a Scotsman, rather than an Englishman, chosen to revise the Maltese Code? Could the reason have been that Scottish lawyers were more attuned to the Roman Law[74] than their English counterparts?

Jameson's biography might provide an answer.[75] According to the husband of a descendant,

> Jameson had the happy trait of making himself immediately agreeable to people on their first acquaintance of him and never subsequently losing their respect. This was certainly the case with [Governor] Sir Henry Bouverie and his Chief Secretary, Sir Hector Greig. On no fewer than four occasions between 24 December 1840 and 11 January 1841, he was invited to dinner by Sir Hector and on another evening by the Governor. This suggests something more than recognition of Andrew Jameson as a congenial companion at the dinner table. The Governor of Malta and the Chief Secretary must have seen in Andrew Jameson a highly appropriate person to revise the Draft Criminal Code of Malta.

The question can be easily overlooked whether an Army Officer (Bouverie) and a Superintendent of Quarantine (Greig) had what it takes to discern a legal drafter's qualifications, since our attention is taken up by the *really* intriguing bit:

> It was not only that he was a competent lawyer but, just as importantly, his qualifications in that profession had been gained in Scotland where the law was based on Roman

73 *Ibid.*, 138.

74 Criminal law was dealt with to a limited extent in Books 47 and 48 of the Digest, which Justinian called *libri terribiles* – STEIN, P (1999): *Roman Law in European History* Cambridge University Press, Cambridge, 106 – but that is not necessarily the "Roman Law" referred to here. We shall return to this point later.

75 More details, including correspondence, can be found in chapters 8 and 10 of GOURLAY, D (2015): *Sheriff Andrew Jameson. The Life of Effie Gray's Uncle* Melrose Books, United Kingdom.

> Civil Law as was that of Malta. Moreover, he was fluent in Italian.[76]

Fluency in Italian was certainly a bonus. But what about the assertion that the law of Scotland "was based on Roman Civil Law"?[77]

Alberto Cadoppi, Professor of Criminal Law, argues that already in 1842, Scots Criminal Law was in certain respects even more Anglo-Saxon than English Criminal Law. On the whole, Scots Criminal Law was '*sostanzialmente diritto penale di* Common Law'[78] and consequently Jameson's observations are to be deemed '*come se fossero state fatte da un qualsiasi criminalista inglese:*

---

76 GOURLAY, D (2009): "Andrew Jameson and the Origins of the Criminal Code of Malta" in *Melita Historica*, Vol. XV, no. 2 The Malta Historical Society, Ħaż-Żabbar, Malta, 114. It would seem pertinent to look further into Jameson's engagement. Let us consider the facts: i. Jameson was invited by the Governor after leaving his visiting card presumably with underlings (as per GOURLAY, D (2010): "Andrew Jameson (1811-1870)" a paper presented at the Conference *Andrew Jameson: a Scottish eye to the Mediterranean Law Experience* organized by the University of Padua and the Robert Gordon University of Aberdeen, in Padua 12-13 March 2010, the text of which Dr Gourlay kindly forwarded to the present author). ii. Jameson was 29 when he met Governor Bouverie. ii. Gourlay tells us (p. 114) that Jameson had come to Malta for health reasons: he suffered from 'a serious throat complaint', dysphonia. iii. Jameson's private practice had been badly hit by this disorder. iv. Jameson returned to Scotland to apply for substitute-Sheriff but somehow was not successful and came back to Malta to do the job for the Governor (p. 117). v. The Dean of the Faculty of Advocates in Edinburgh seems to have been a friend both of Jameson and of Chief Secretary Greig (p. 118). At this juncture, it seems legitimate to ask whether Bouverie (and/or Greig) and Jameson were Freemasons, and if this possible commonality could have paved the way for the meeting and eventual commission. We are not being judgmental here about their possible belonging to the brotherhood, save perhaps for the fact that it would seem that it was not open to the Maltese. However, it must be recorded that the present author has emailed Dr Gourlay who very kindly indicated that nothing found in Jameson's papers indicates he belonged to a Lodge. Despite this lack of documentary evidence, the present author does not deem it reasonable to rule out the question's legitimacy.

77 The author, Dr Douglas Gourlay, 'graduated with degrees in History from the University of St Andrews, Scotland, and spent seven years in the engineering industry before transferring to business education' (p. 109), so perhaps we should look elsewhere for an answer to this question.

78 [common-law Criminal Law].

insomma, da un common lawyer'.[79] Where Jameson proposes his opinions,

> *bisogna avere l'accortezza di valutare le opinioni dell'avvocato edinense tenendo presente l'origine scozzese delle teoriche da lui esposte. [...N]ella loro 'matrice giuridico-culturale', nel DNA di riferimento, queste peculiarità dottrinali scozzesi non si discostano poi troppo dai fondamenti dello stesso diritto inglese.*[80]

Is it reasonable not to presume that Jameson had self-promoted himself? In a letter to Greig,[81] Jameson championed his own cause saying, 'Our studies and pursuits [in Scotland], being necessarily more connected with the Roman Law and the foreign codes, which are founded upon that great monument of ancient wisdom as well as with general Jurisprudence, dispose us to take a greater interest in such improvements as that which you are now engaged in [...]'.[82]

Bonavita was irked by his work being submitted to Jameson's appraisal for at least two reasons. First, Jameson received remuneration while he, Bonavita, did not. Secondly, and to our mind more importantly, because he considered Jameson '*un avvocato oscuro*'[83] whose tone was at times '*insolente*'.[84] Bonavita's summing up of the situation is corroborated by Dr Gourlay himself:

---

79 CADOPPI, *op. cit.*, XCVII. [as if made by an English Criminal lawyer: in other words, a Common Lawyer].

80 *Ibid.*, XCVIII. [one has to be aware of the need to evaluate the Edinburgh advocate's opinions in the light of the Scottish origins of the notions he proffers. The 'juridico-cultural matrix', the reference DNA, of these Scottish doctrines are not at all distant from the very bases of English law].

81 11 June 1842.

82 GOURLAY, *op. cit.*, 118. This strategy seems to have worked on Greig, whose knowledge of the law must have been impressionistic at best. In fact, in a letter of 25 June, Grieg tells Jameson that if the Colonial Office 'decide[s] that an English lawyer is to make the report I am certain that the result will not be satisfactory for want of acquaintance with the Roman Law' – quoted by GOURLAY, *op. cit.*, 119. Later on, however, we shall see how Jameson rejects the utility of Roman Law to the Criminal Law.

83 [an obscure advocate].

84 [insolent].

"in 1841 [Jameson was still] not known outside a small coterie of legal friends and acquaintances in Edinburgh."[85] Bonavita did not display the reaction of a proud, bigoted provincial lawyer. He was a brilliant man who felt humiliated when a lesser but more powerful individual revised his work.[86]

4.2 Scots Law and Roman Law

What about the much hallowed Roman Law qualities of Scots Law? Does Maltese law belong to the same Roman Law tradition which "inspires" Scots Law?

In his report, Jameson himself makes his views on Roman Law amply clear:

> It is a matter of notoriety that the Roman Laws, notwithstanding their deserved celebrity in the matter of civil rights and obligations contain many objectionable doctrines and arbitrary provisions in respect to crimes.[87]

Despite this manifest rejection of Roman Law by the Scottish reviser of the Draft Code, there is a persistent idea that Scots Law - through its Roman Law connection - is useful to Maltese Criminal Law.

Admittedly, Jameson's report carries a reference to the 'right in private individuals to prosecute criminally in case of the Crown Advocate refusing to prosecute'. However a telling qualification follows: 'This is a part of the Scottish system, which

---

85 GOURLAY, *op. cit.*, 113.

86 In Cadoppi's words (CADOPPI, *op. cit.*, CXXIII): '*illustri giuristi erano costretti a compilare un codice «nazionale» sotto l'occhiuta supervisione di «oscuri avvocati» che, a loro vantaggio, avevano il solo fatto di appartenere all'etnia dominante l'isola sotto il profilo politico-militare*' [illustrious jurists were bound to compile a "national" code under the watchful supervision of "obscure advocates" whose only advantage was that they belonged to the politically and militarily dominant ethnicity on the island]. Governor Bouverie knew that Bonavita would 'naturally be jealous' of Jameson, but seems not to have given a second thought to the fact that he (Bouverie) would expect him (Bonavita) to 'give [Jameson] any Explanation, which [Jameson might] require' - letter dated September 1842 from Bouverie to Jameson quoted by GOURLAY, *op. cit.*, 125.

87 JAMESON, *op. cit.*, 133.

in this respect is formed on the same principles, as that in Malta [emphasis added]'.[88]

4.2.1 The Roman Law connection

Professor Peter Stein tells us that 'it was usual [...] for budding Scots lawyers to study civil law on the continent, at first in France and from the late sixteenth century in the Netherlands'.[89] During the 1970s, a number of Scottish Law Commission memoranda made active reference to Roman-Dutch law.[90]

The Scots Law of the past drew from the Roman-Dutch well. As regards the present, a 1992 essay paints another picture:

> The teaching of Roman Law in [Scottish] universities has declined. [...] On reading the speeches in [certain] cases [...] one gains a faint impression that the English Lords of Appeal know more about Roman Law than most Scots lawyers do. This sad decline causes surprises both to Scottish practitioners and to foreign lawyers.[91]

Writing nine years later, Professor Reinhard Zimmermann describes the assurgent prestige of English law in Scotland:

> In the second half of the nineteenth century [...] Scotland became [...] a somewhat backward province of the United Kingdom, and the level of the native legal culture, and legal education, descended to an equally low level. [Lawyers] no longer went on the grand tour to France or Holland, but to the Inns of Court in London. After the industrial revolution, England offered more attractive career possibilities due to its extended trade empire. As England's prestige grew, so did that of the Common Law. Its influence in Scotland became

---

88 *Ibid.*, 144.

89 STEIN, *op. cit.*, 87.

90 CAREY MILLER, DL (1992): 'Systems of Property: Grotius and Stair' in CAREY MILLER, DL & MEYERS, DW (EDS.): *Comparative and Historical Essays in Scots Law* Butterworths & The Law Society of Scotland, Edinburgh, 13.

91 WILSON, WA (1992): 'The Importance of Analysis' in CAREY MILLER, DL & MEYERS, DW (EDS.): *Comparative and Historical Essays in Scots Law* Butterworths & The Law Society of Scotland, Edinburgh, 171.

> increasingly perceptible, as long as legal discourse ventured beyond the mosses and muirs of the Scottish highlands.[92]

Discussing the making of Scots Law, authors OF Robinson, TD Fergus, and Professor WM Gordon state that:

> Although Scots law is not, as is sometimes popularly believed, based entirely on Roman Law, one of the major influences in its formative years, along with feudal and canon law, was the Roman system in the shape of its revived civilian tradition. [...] Yet important though Roman law in its developed mediaeval form undoubtedly was, its influence can be exaggerated. The use of Roman terminology does not necessarily indicate the adoption of a Roman institution [...] Roman law has never been of itself authoritative in Scotland. Rather, as in the *pays de coutumes*, the civil law was received because of its rational character and as a source of equitable principle when the native law was silent or obscure. This is made plain in the work of the early Scottish institutional writers who were the first to reflect on the content of Scots law. Sir Thomas Craig wrote that "we in this kingdom are bound by the laws of the Romans insofar as they are in harmony with the laws of nature and right reason" (*Ius feudale*, I,2,14).[93]

With this caveat clearly in sight, these three authors turn their attention specifically to Criminal Law. While Malta's Caruana Dingli was translating Carmignani's *Elementi del Diritto Criminale*,[94] Scotland was following the "almost solitary light to

---

92 ZIMMERMANN, R (2001): *Roman Law, Contemporary Law, European Law. The Civilian Tradition Today* Oxford University Press, Oxford, 152-153.

93 ROBINSON, OF, FERGUS, TD, GORDON, WM (2000): *European Legal History* Butterworths, London-Edinburgh-Dublin, 14.1.1. These three authors teach or taught at the University of Glasgow.

94 Published in 1847-48 on Malta. In 1863, a second, revised edition was published in Milan. For more details, see MANGION, R. (2009), "Professors who Taught International Law within the Faculty of Laws, University of Malta" in MARTINEZ GUTIÉRREZ, N.A. (ED.), *Serving the Rule of International Law: Essays in Honour of Professor David Joseph Attard*, Mare Nostrum Publications, Malta, 33-37.

guide [her] course over the [...] criminal jurisprudence":[95] Baron David Hume. Robinson *et al* have this to say:

> In the sphere of criminal law there are two important works which are generally regarded as institutional in the sense of carrying authority. The first is Mackenzie's *The Laws and Customs of Scotland in Matters Criminal* (1678) [...] Important in its day, and for basic principles, it is no longer regularly consulted since, for example, treason is largely described in straightforwardly Roman terms [...] The second is Baron Hume's *Commentaries on the Law of Scotland respecting Crimes* (1797). [...S]ignificantly, he states that in the absence of native authority he has looked to England rather than to Rome, in that English society offers a better model in an area of law where social habits have an important influence. Hume is still of considerable authority, being regularly cited both in court and in the literature.[96]

The authorities Robinson *et al* refer to are important because, as Professor TH Jones and MGA Christie point out:

> Unlike many European countries [...] and the USA [...] there is no criminal code in Scotland. [...] Equally there is no authorised account of the principles which govern the operation of the criminal law. It follows that this area of the law is less certain [...] in Scotland than may be the case elsewhere.[97]

Roman Law does not feature in these authors' enumeration of the sources of Scots Criminal Law.[98] The reason could be that, to borrow Professor Christopher Gane's words, 'Hume was able to reject Roman Law as a source of [Scottish] Criminal Law'.[99]

---

95 ANON. (1844): 'A Supplement to Hume's Commentaries on the Law of Scotland respecting Crimes' in *The North British Review*, Vol. IV, November 1845-February 1846 WP Kennedy, Edinburgh, 313.

96 ROBINSON ET AL, *op. cit.*, 14.2.11.

97 JONES, TH & CHRISTIE, MGA (2003): *Greens Concise Scots Law Criminal Law* 3rd ed. Thomson, Edinburgh, 11.

98 *Op. cit.*, Chapter 3.

99 GANE, C (2005): 'Civilian and English influences on Scots Criminal Law' in REID, E, ET AL (EDS.): *A Mixed Legal System in Transition. TB Smith and the Progress*

The post-Hume scenario was thus depicted by Professor Sir Gerald H. Gordon:

> There has been no extended discussion of the principles of Scots criminal law since Hume's *Commentaries*. Alison merely repeats Hume with the addition of a few English cases; Anderson is a very brief treatment and avoids discussion; Macdonald is little more than a convenient digest, and is confused and inaccurate. The only systematic modern treatment is that contained in three comparatively short chapters of Professor Smith's *Short Commentary*.[100]

Sir Thomas B. Smith (1915-1988) was a Scottish nationalist professor, whose ideas were controversial but highly influential. To his *Commentary* can be attributed the paternity of the suggestion that 'the Roman association has been of first importance in assisting the development of a corpus of Scottish criminal law independent of English law'.[101]

However, Professor Gane refutes Smith's weighty suggestion. *Inter alia*, he shows that in the hundred years preceding his own (2005) essay, the High Court of Justiciary 'referred to Roman Law on only seven occasions.'[102] He asserts that very few offences have a 'clearly identifiable Roman law origin', the clearest two being *plagium* (child-stealing) and violation of sepulchres; in both cases contemporary Scots Law has 'departed significantly from their historical origins and modern accounts of them make no reference to their background in Roman law.'[103]

4.2.2 The English Law connection

Gane offers more insight: 'English law was an established influence

---

of Scots Law Edinburgh University Press, Edinburgh, 223.

100 GORDON, GH (1967): *The Criminal Law of Scotland* 1st ed., W Green & Son Ltd/Scottish Universities Law Institute, Edinburgh, 3-4.

101 SMITH, TB (1962): *Short Commentary on the Law of Scotland* W Green, Edinburgh, 119.

102 GANE, *op. cit.*, 227.

103 *Ibid.*

on Scots criminal law long before Hume's time'[104] even though 'it is only rarely [...] that one finds explicit references to English law or practice in the reports of proceedings in criminal cases before the Union with England.'[105] This notwithstanding, studies have shown 'striking examples of apparent borrowing'[106] from English law. Explicit reference to English writers and judicial decisions appear 'very quickly after the Union' when 'Scottish advocates quickly got into the way of citing English authority.'[107] Then, in the 'post-Union era', 'Scottish courts, untrammelled by a Civilian history or an English future, largely ignored both influences.'[108]

Gane concludes that while it may 'at one time' have been the case that the Roman association was of first importance in the development of Scots criminal law, 'this is certainly no longer the case':[109]

> For a variety of reasons, modern Scots criminal law is applied and developed in a way which is effectively cut off from its Civilian [i.e., Roman Law] history. [...] The independence of Scots Law is in large measure attributable to Hume's rejection of both the Civil [i.e., Roman] Law and English Law as sources of Scots Law [...] Finally, there is the suggestion that it was in the post-Hume period that English influence began to be felt. But that too must be rejected. There is clear evidence of early, significant and long-lasting English influence in the criminal law.[110]

For the above reasons, it would seem that claims about Scots Law's usefulness to Maltese Criminal Law are beyond the shadow of a doubt, a myth.[111]

104 GANE, *op. cit.*, 228.

105 *Ibid.*, 229.

106 *Idem.*

107 *Ibid.*, 230.

107 *Op. cit.*, 232.

109 *Op. cit.*, 238.

109 *Ibid.*

111 The foremost champion of this idea seems to be former Chief Justice Vincent de Gaetano. As we have already seen, Professor Cadoppi makes it amply clear that '*alla metà dell'Ottocento la Scottish law era senza dubbio assai più vicina a quella inglese che a quella continentale. [...] Va però chiarito [...] che, nonostante la 'nomea' di diritto di natura 'mista' (di* civil law *e di* Common Law) *della Scottish*

4.3 Roman Law in Malta

De Bono puts it neatly when he says that the applicable Roman Law (*ius commune*) in Malta was not what we find in the *Corpus iuris* but what was modified by the Canon Law, explained by the authors and received by the Courts.[112] This strain of "Roman Law" – the Romanist tradition as received in Italy[113] – is different to the Roman-Dutch tradition. Recounting the legal history of Western Europe would be far beyond the scope of this essay, and the reader is invited to refer to the numerous books available on the subject.[114] Suffice it to say, however, that Roman-Dutch law[115] – i.e., the "Roman Law" which influenced Scots Law – is the law of Holland

---

(criminal) law, *in realtà essa è oggi, ed era già nel 1842, sostanzialmente diritto penale di* Common Law' [from the mid-19th century, Scottish law was undoubtedly closer to English than to Continental law. However, it has to be clarified that despite the notoriety of the hybrid nature (i.e., a melange of civil and Common Law) of Scottish (criminal) law, in reality nowadays, as was the case already in 1842, it is substantially a Common Law Criminal Law] – CADOPPI, *op. cit.* 2003, XCVII. Cadoppi's words acquire new significance because, as he himself acknowledges (CADOPPI, *op. cit.* 2003, LXXXIII), he was expressly invited to the University of Malta in 1994 by none other than His Lordship Dr Vincent de Gaetano. In November 2012, that is after the initial publication of this essay in *Id-Dritt*, Dr de Gaetano published a paper called "Social Rights in Malta – An Overview" ("a slightly modified version of a paper commissioned by Professor Julia Iliopoulos-Strangas in connection with the forthcoming edition of her work on the Protection of Social Rights in Europe"). He wrote, "In spite of the influence of Roman law on Scots law, the latter has had very little, if any, direct influence on Maltese law. Nevertheless Scottish case-law and text-writers remain useful for purposes of interpretation even in such unlikely areas as the general principles of criminal law and criminal liability." In the light of what has been brought to the fore in the present essay, the present author is of the opinion that the underlying logic of Dr de Gaetano's statement is convoluted at best.

112 '*Anche Baldo aveva scritto: Omnes populi possunt facere sibi statuta, et ubi cessat statutum habet locum ius civile (Ad L. 7, Dig. de inst. et iure). Si avverta, però, che il diritto comune, al quale si rapporta il codice, è meno quello che risulta dai testi del Corpus iuris, che quello che fu modificato dal diritto canonico, esposto dagli scrittori e ricevuto dall'uso del foro.*' – DE BONO, *op. cit.*, 211.

113 '*Romanistica-italiana*' [Roman(istic)-Italian] says CADOPPI, *op. cit.*, XC-XCI.

114 The present author prefers the works of Paolo Grossi and Randall Lesaffer, but there are many others available in English, Italian and French, the top three foreign languages in which the average Maltese is fluent.

115 *Rooms-Hollands Recht*. The term was coined by Dutch legal scholar Simon van Leeuwen (1626-82).

expressed in Roman terms.[116] There *are* similarities, of course. Grotius,[117] though a Protestant and a humanist, accepted the ideas of the *Secunda Scholastica* and of Thomas Aquinas, the foremost Catholic and mediaeval thinker. *But* he 'reinterpreted them with originality and set them within his own comprehensive, synthetic, and systematic vision of the law'.[118] To equate the Roman-Dutch law to the Italian tradition prevailing in Malta at the time of the compilation of the Criminal Code and possibly today would be very difficult.

5. Attitudes and ideology

5.1 Different underlying philosophies

Real differences have been observed between the philosophies underlying the Italian and North European approaches to Criminal Law. Cadoppi argues that the Common Law holds to the "sacredness of life"[119] even more strongly than the Italian tradition, as it punishes homicide more harshly.

Furthermore, he indicates that Anglo-Saxon countries perceive culpability and *mens rea* in an 'ethicising' fashion[120] and the offender's wickedness becomes all-important. In the Italian tradition this aspect is perhaps less marked, as Italian law is more

---

116 Professor Cavanna tells us that it was '*una creatura originale, che stava allo sbocco del processo di recezione del diritto comune nelle province settentrionali dei Paesi Bassi: era un prodotto nuovo, scaturito da una nazionalizzazione giurisprudenziale del diritto comune nella prassi olandese*' [an original creation, produced by the process of reception of the *ius commune* in the northern provinces of the Low Countries: it was a new product, born from the jurisprudential nationalisation of the *ius commune* received in Dutch practice]. – CAVANNA, A (1982): *Storia del Diritto Moderno in Europa. Le fonti e il pensiero giuridico* Giuffrè editore, Milan, 437-438.

117 Hugo Grotius († 1645) is considered the "father of Roman-Dutch Law". (This opinion is however not universally shared – *vide* BAUMAN, R A (1983): "Grotius: Father of Roman-Dutch Law?" in 1983 *Bull. Austl. Soc. Leg. Phil.*, no. 26 Australian Society of Legal Philosophy, Canberra 1983.)

118 BELLOMO, M (TRS. COCHRANE, L) (1995): *The Common Legal Past of Europe* The Catholic University of America Press, Washington D.C., 233.

119 Jameson uses the same phrase: 'In the Law of England and of Scotland the sacredness of human safety and life...' –JAMESON, *op. cit.*, 118.

120 [*concezione «eticizzante»*].

interested in the harm caused than the agent's subjective nature, disposition and temperament. The discourse is probably linked to the fact that Italian law is more *objectivistic* than *subjectivistic* when compared to the Anglo-Saxon and other North European traditions.[121]

However, when one philosophy is considered *better* than the other, the context changes from the Criminal Law to Anthropology. Notions of an anthropological nature condition how the Maltese of today view the Criminal Code and whether they are ready to accept myths as facts.[122]

5.2 Attitudes

At the turning point between the 18th and 19th centuries, Malta found herself in a tug-of-war between France and Britain, embroiled as they were in eastbound European imperialism. From this commonality sprang a shared worldview: Orientalism.[123]

The myths surrounding the Criminal Code are best understood if we bear in mind that:

---

121 CADOPPI, *op. cit.*, CXIX. This is a field of inquiry which, it goes without saying, lies much beyond the scope of the present essay.

122 This phenomenon is treated by Professor Theodore KODITSCHEK in his *Liberalism, Imperialism, and the Historical Imagination* (Cambridge University Press, New York 2011). 'He shows how both imperialists and the imperialized were drawn to reflect back on Empire's past as a result of the need to construct a modern, multinational British imperial identity for a more economically expansive and enlightened present. [...] Koditschek illuminates the way in which discourse altered practice, and vice versa ...' – book's blurb.

123 SAID, EW (2003 ed.): *Orientalism* Penguin, London, 4: 'Orientalism derives from a particular closeness experienced between Britain and France and the Orient, which until the early nineteenth century had really meant only India and the Bible lands. From the beginning of the nineteenth century until the end of World War II, France and Britain dominated the Orient and Orientalism'. This is not to say that Orientalism was exclusive to these two countries. Turinese Davide BERTOLOTTI, for instance, writes '*La prima calata degli Arabi in Sicilia è pure la prima menzione che faccian le storie della comparsa di questi Barbari orientali sulle spiagge italiane*' ['The first landing of the Arabs in Sicily is also the first time historians mention the appearance of these Oriental barbarians on Italian shores'] (*Gli Arabi in Italia* Baglione, Turin 1838, 22).

(i) the imperialist agenda included the 'civilizing mission'.[124]

Assuming Jameson's mentality was typical of his times, was he being disingenuous when, while on the subject of child prostitution, he wrote that 'the loose morals of the South of Europe have created a necessity for restraining by penal sanctions this vile and profligate traffic'?[125] Was he really unaware of the situation back home?[126]

Not for nothing does Said argue, convincingly, that Sir Walter Scott's novels[127] – *international* best-sellers during the period under review – conveyed the attitude of 'airy condescension' of the Christian/Westerner *vis-à-vis* the Saracen/Oriental.[128]

To Jameson's eye, for instance, the Maltese were 'of an inoffensive and mild character' and lacking 'the strength of either mental or physical constitution which is usually required

---

124 This attitude still pervades "Western fundamentalism". French Professor Alain Supiot gives us an overview of fundamentalism's three forms: (a) Messianism: 'The messianic approach [...] consists of [...] a Text revealed by 'developed' societies to 'developing' ones, leaving the latter no choice but to 'catch up' and convert to modernity.' – SUPIOT, A (TRS. BROWN, S) (2007): *Homo Juridicus. On the Anthropological Function of the Law* Verso, London-New York, 193. (b) Particularism: 'At the opposite extreme, there are those who consider [the Text to] have been revealed to the West alone, such that liberty, equality and democracy would be senseless for other civilizations.' – *Ibid.*, 195. (c) Scientism: 'The "true laws" of human behaviour that are revealed to us by a fetishized science.' – *Ibid.*, 197.

125 JAMESON, *op. cit.*, 69.

126 Indeed he was aware, as further on (p. 76) he refers to the English notion of kidnapping, i.e., 'the stealing and carrying away or secreting of children' also 'with the view of compelling [...] carnal connection'. But it seems he did not consider the kidnapping of children for carnal connection in England as a "vile and profligate traffic" caused by "loose morals". (The reader may wish to refer to at least three books to get the picture: MAHOOD, L (1900): *The Magdalenes. Prostitution in the Nineteenth Century* Routledge, London, JACKSON, LA (2000): *Child Sexual Abuse in Victorian England* Routledge, Oxford, and PORTER, R (1991): *English Society in the Eighteenth Century* Penguin Books, London, particularly p. 270).

127 'One of the most striking features of the new orientalism [i.e., geared toward the legitimization of imperialism] was the extent to which it was dominated by Scots.' – KODITSCHEK, *op. cit.*, 66.

128 SAID, *op. cit.*, 101.

for the commission of even very atrocious crimes';[129]

and

(ii) the British perceived the Maltese as a 'people of Oriental extraction'.[130] Even when the Maltese elicited otherwise positive reactions, the association was always with the Orient:

> the Maltese are neither a rude nor an unpolished people; on the contrary, their manners are in general conciliating, unassuming and obliging. [...] The Maltese are also a more industrious set than the natives of most of the neighbouring countries; though it must at the same time be confessed that *they are rather Jewish in their dealings.*[131]

After all,

> [w]hen the term *Orient* was not simply a synonym for the Asiatic East as a whole [...] it was most rigorously understood as applying to the Islamic Orient. [...] Certainly this was the case in Europe through the middle of the eighteenth century [...] Until that time cultural memory

129 JAMESON, *op. cit.*, 29. Was he being disingenuous, had he been hoodwinked by the representatives of the descendants of corsair galley crews and Great Siege combatants and ancestors of the heroes of World War II, or did he mistake the diffidence and savoir faire of the Maltese bourgeois for effeteness?

130 BIGELOW, A (1831): *Travels in Malta and Sicily: with sketches of Gibraltar in 1827* Carter, Hendee & Babcock, Boston, 124.

131 [emphasis added] ANON. (1806): 'Remarks on Malta and Sicily' in *The Monthly Magazine*, Vol. XX. Richard Phillips, London, 515. Jameson believed wholeheartedly in the "otherness" of the Maltese, as exemplified by this excerpt: 'the excuse of instantaneous passion seems to be so dangerous among a southern race and so contrary to the sound principles of criminal responsibility'. – JAMESON, *op. cit.*, 120. Ironically – but Jameson seems to be blind to this irony – the "excuse of instantaneous passion" he tells us 'seems to have been derived from the Bavarian and other German Codes' (p. 120). Now he is either writing tongue-in-cheek (to please his reader, the Secretary of State?) or else he is oblivious to the glaring contradiction. Since when are Germans a "southern race"? Unless of course, he is now equating Catholic Germans with the southern race. Prejudice always bore muddled thinking. On this particular subject, Jameson tells us that where provocation is concerned, 'the Laws of these two divisions of Great Britain [*viz.* England and Scotland] greatly differ [...] perhaps more than in any other [branch of practice] which involves general principles. The Law of Scotland demands more self command in cases of inconsiderable wrong. It admits no excuse from mere rage or heat of blood unless occasioned "by some adequate and serious cause [...]"' (p. lxxviii).

> gave understandable prominence to such relatively distant events as [...] the conquest of Sicily [...][132]

Sicily was therefore "Oriental".[133] Lord Bentinck, writing in 1812, considered Sicily a degraded society.[134] Naples was viewed as the foretaste of the Orient.[135] Should we expect a different attitude with regard to Malta?[136] For the French historian Dominic Miège,

---

132 SAID, *op. cit.*, 75.

133 One could go one step further. Writing as recently as 1994, F.H. Stewart (STEWART, FH (1994): *Honor* University of Chicago Press, Chicago-London, 76) feels he has to remark that Muslim rule ended in Sicily in the 11th century, in Spain in the 15th, and in the Balkans in the 19th and 20th, and therefore 'the Muslims surely left their stamp on these areas in one way or another'. But this argument is fallacious. Let us consider Sicily. In 1090, the Normans took Sicily from the Arabs, and later on, Lombard (and Piedmontese) settlers poured in. (See QUATRIGLIO, G (1996, 1999): *Mille Anni in Sicilia. Dagli Arabi ai Borboni* Marsilio, Venice, 14-15.) Why doesn't the stamp left by these Germanic peoples affect Sicily's profile? What makes the Muslim presence more important than the Germanic presence in the assessment of Sicily's "Oriental character"?

134 ROSSELLI, *op. cit.*, 116.

135 See the excerpt from Compagna's speech quoted at the very beginning of this essay.

136 A characteristic of Professor Mario Vella's style is his penchant for dovetailing brilliant but seemingly unrelated historico-anthropological analyses to his desired conclusions. True to form, in an essay on economic development (VELLA, M (2009): 'The economics of hypocrisy – deconstructing half a century of development discourse in Malta – notes on work in progress' in CASSAR, G *ET AL* (EDS.): *Social Transitions in Maltese Society*, Agenda, Ħal Luqa, Malta, 363-364), he proffers a confirmation that this British attitude toward the Maltese percolated down to the 20th century. Vella remarks that Mintoff's 'refusal to play according to [British] "gentlemanly" rules was interpreted by both adversaries and admirers in Britain and elsewhere either as the effect of an obnoxious personality [...] or as the manifestation of regional (Levantine) cultural characteristics. [...] Rather than attempting to understand the vocabulary and the grammar of his unorthodox game, they simply labelled it as evidence of his otherness and interpreted his otherness as evidence of an aggressiveness associated with a lower stage of social evolution, one that is more direct and in-your-face because it is unencumbered by the refined etiquette of the more advanced civilizations.' Vella reminds us that Said 'identified laziness as one of the tropes of Orientalism; the oriental is, in the perception of the Western, lazy and incompetent but may deviously spring up when one least expects him to and do harm. If Mintoff represented the devious trope in London's Orientalist perception of Malta, Borg Olivier represented the other face of the oriental Janus. [...] From this Orientalist perspective, a perspective shared both by Conservatives and Labour in Britain, the "Maltese" were both hyperactively devious and indolently incompetent.'

consul in Valletta in the 1830s, the Maltese character had a strain of Oriental fatalism.[137]

5.3 Ideology

J.S. Mill put it politely: 'Englishmen are not always incapable of shaking off insular prejudices, and governing another country according to its wants, and not according to common English habits and notions.'[138]

Imperialist ideology spurred Stoddart's insistence in 1828 that Maltese lawyers should learn English in order to interpret according to their proper principles the new laws of Malta which were either copied from English statutes or else drawn up according to the English spirit.[139]

This was all new to the Maltese, who up till then had been accustomed to be ruled by the *ius commune*, Romano-Canonical Law, and Sicilian and Maltese usages[140] expressed in Italian. The old way was the "natural" way;[141] the new way consisted of the importation of English laws through the codification process[142]

137 GREGORY, D (1996): *Malta, Britain and the European Powers, 1793-1815* Associated University Presses, Inc., Cranbury, New Jersey, 33. Gregory cites more contemporary descriptions of the Maltese (*vide* pp. 31-33).

138 MILL, JS (1868/1982): *England and Ireland*, Collected Works, Vol. VI Toronto University Press, Toronto, 519.

139 NOVARESE, D (2003): 'Istanze costituzionali e codificazione a Malta nel secolo XIX. Le origini del codice penale del 1854' in VINCIGUERRA (ED.), *Leggi Criminali per l'Isola di Malta e Sue Dipendenze (1854)*. CEDAM, Padua, LI.

140 *Dritto Municipale di Malta Compilato Sotto De Rohan G.M. Or Nuovamente Corredato di Annotazioni* (1841) Francesco Cumbo, Malta, Tome I, XII.

141 As De Caro put it, 'Our legislation is not the work of one man, one century, one hand.' – DE CARO, A (1845): *Il Processo Criminale in Malta* Valletta, 126. [*La nostra legislazione scritta non è opra di un sol uomo, d'un sol secolo, d'una mano*] This beautiful axiom refers to the compilation of laws in the *Ancien Régime*, as distinct from the "new" law-making technique of abstraction.

142 This complex idea goes beyond the scope of the present essay but probably to the root of the mixed (Common Law-Civil Law) law-making system, namely, the codification (a Civil-Law idea) of the Common Law. The contention at the time was not the codification process *per se* of a Common Law (or, during the Order's rule, of the *ius commune*), but the wholesale importation of English rules. As a parallel we can recall the quarrel, at the time of the compilation of the Municipal Code, between the Maltese jurists and the Apulian Giandonato Rogadeo, the compiler who hailed

and the concomitant "invitation" to learn English to understand their spirit and principles. Those were times steeped in an ideology which believed, or wanted to believe, that colonies derived great good from being British possessions. After all, as Scotsman GF Leckie put it, 'while France conquers to devastate, Britain conquers to do good'.[143]

When the Maltese drafters admitted that their project was modelled on the Code of the Two Sicilies, albeit with innovative solutions added, their position elicited Stoddart's sarcasm. He dismissed it as '*ombra dell'ombra di un Maggior Pianeta*'.[144]

This was the same Stoddart who, in the face of the legal confusion caused also by the Common Law scions engrafted upon Malta's juridical system,[145] stated, 'It is another advantage of the project Code that it will supersede and annul the greater part of the old Laws, and will tend to introduce more certainty, consistency and simplicity into the administration of Justice in criminal matters.'[146]

---

from Naples, because they deemed his provisions did not reflect the temperament of the Maltese nation (CIAPPARA, F (2006): *Enlightenment and Reform in Malta 1740-1798* Midsea Books, Santa Venera, Malta, 66). In other words, it was the nationality of the rules which irked the Maltese both under the Order and the British, rather than the codification process itself. Nowadays, aspirations have been turned on their head: the Maltese – like other post-colonial peoples – want to make theirs the laws of their former colonial masters. *Vide* KOSKENNIEMI, M (2004): *The Gentle Civilizer of Nations. The Rise and Fall of International Law 1870-1960* Cambridge University Press, Cambridge, *passim* for a deeper analysis.

143 Leckie wrote the influential Historical Survey of the Foreign Affairs of Great Britain, with a view to explain the causes of the disasters of the late and present wars (1808). Quoted by ROSSELLI, *op. cit.*, 117.

144 DE CARO, *op. cit.* 1845, 93 fn. 2. [shadow of the shadow of a Major Planet].

145 The first forty years of the British presence were marked by an '*incessante ma assai poco coordinata introduzione normativa ispirata a istituti di Common Law, continuamente contrappuntata da provvedimenti intesi a ovviare ai problemi contingenti innescati da questa stessa produzione*' [incessant but poorly coordinated legislative production inspired by Common Law notions and counterpoised by measures meant to offset contingent problems sparked by this very same production] which then ended up creating '*una situazione di confusione e di incertezza tanto nella giustizia penale che in quella civile*' [a situation of confusion and uncertainty both in the penal and civil field] – DEZZA, *op. cit.* 2003, CCCX.

146 Quoted by NOVARESE, *op. cit.* 2003, LVII.

In the light of this facet of the dominant ideology of the times, Bonavita's quest for a system which was at once open to receive Common Law rules and principles while respecting Civil-Law Maltese traditions and specifities, takes on new meaning. Bonavita fought, and won, against the exponents of the most obtuse imperialist and colonialist mentality of the British Administration.[147]

5.4 Power and prejudice

For Jameson, there was no need to substantiate the claim that 'the circumstances and feelings of society [on the Ionian Islands] must be nearly similar to those of Malta'.[148] He took it for granted that his readers would share his prejudice that the Mediterraneans are "others", and therefore uncouth and on the fringes of civilization. A Briton, John Galt, who visited Malta in 1809, recorded that 'most resident English treated the Maltese with contempt, and were jealous of the way the administration went out of its way to conciliate the natives'.[149]

In 1994, FH Stewart still felt bound to concede that 'it is undoubtedly true that the peoples of southern Europe, and especially the rural peoples, resemble in some ways those of the Levant and North Africa more than they do those of northern Europe'.[150] But, significantly he counterargues, busting another myth in the process, that

> the attempts [...] to characterize these resemblances have not, however, been very happy. Pitt-Rivers [...], for instance, mentions among "the general structural characteristics of the Mediterranean communities: their moral cohesiveness and the absence of contrast between town and country which was so important in England and northern Europe." I see no reason to believe that "moral cohesiveness," whatever that may be, is or was any more common in (say) Moroc-

147 DEZZA, *op. cit.* 2003, CCCXIII.

148 JAMESON, *op. cit.*, 117. Jameson's argument is an obvious converse fallacy of accident.

149 GREGORY, *op. cit.*, 32.

150 STEWART, *op. cit.*, 75.

> can communities than in Norwegian ones. As for the contrast between town and country, it has long been extremely marked in much of North Africa and the Levant; there is no reason to believe that it is less marked than in northern Europe, and considerable evidence (e.g., from dialectology) that it is more marked.[151]

In other words, the whole issue boils down to 'timeworn prejudices about southern European "others"'. Already in the nineteenth century Tylor[152] had considered Mediterraneans as less civilized than northern Europeans because of their need to gesture while speaking, rather than conveying their message in plain language.'[153] From these prejudices sprouted a "truth" a psychologist once described as 'the fallacy of taking as absolute values [one's] own preferred values'[154] and an anthropologist described as:

---

151 *Ibid.*, 75, fn. 5.

152 Sir Edward Burnett Tylor (1832-1917) was an English anthropologist.

153 STEWART, CH (2002): 'The Mediterranean as a culture area' in BARNARD, A & J. SPENCER, J (EDS.), *Encyclopedia of Social and Cultural anthropology* Routledge, London, 324. Jameson shares this prejudice: 'Nobody who has witnessed the quarrels of the lower orders – or heard the language, they are in the habit on such occasions of using to one another [did Jameson know Maltese?] will be slow to see the danger of allowing this cause of provocation to be admitted. The habits of Southern Nations are still more prone to this species of insult, and their languages usually more copious in terms of reproach and derision. To this their vivacity and dramatic turn, adds the use of insulting gesture and mimicry'. – JAMESON, *op. cit.*, lxxix. Thankfully, Oscar Wilde and Rowan Atkinson's Blackadder corrected that misapprehension.

154 SAPIR, E (1993 ed.): *The Psychology of Culture* Mouten de Guyter, Berlin, 64. In 2002, a book was published which classified the Maltese as 'ambivalent Europeans', among other things because they are (or were at the time) practising Roman Catholics (i.e., an unreformed brand of Christianity, i.e., not conducive to the ethic leading to/necessary for capitalism). *Vide* MITCHELL, JP (2002): *Ambivalent Europeans. Ritual, Memory and the Public Sphere in Malta* Routledge, London, *passim*. This author, who hails from the north-westernmost margins of Europe, i.e. Britain, titled the first chapter of his book, 'Malta on the Margins of Europe: A history of ambivalence' probably because Malta is on the southernmost margins of Europe! Yet, does he not consider himself, and all the Nordic peoples, 'ambivalent Europeans' (whatever that may mean) because they are on the other (i.e., north-western and northern) margins of Europe? Not only the geographical margins, but also the historical margins. What is ambivalent about Maltese history but not about British history? That Malta was under Muslim rule a thousand years back? Weren't the northern tribes and peoples going through the "dark ages" a thousand years back, when they were still outside the "Romanized world"? Isn't one key to interpret

> The particular "textual attitude" of the Orientalist produces an influential version of "knowledge" which achieves the status of truth by virtue of the cultural power of the knower. Such "truth" becomes an infinite rehearsal of tropes such as exoticism, mystery, cunning, deviousness, which all place the Oriental as the other of Europe.[155]

The prejudices – the "truth" – inflamed the rationalization of imperialism as holding the moral high ground 'on the basis of a notion of cultural progress, with [the imperialist's] own culture representing a stage of advancement.' But 'to compare cultures on such a scale would be to assert that we have [...] objective, concrete criteria. Many questions we ask about culture thus are naïve and blind in that we think we are connected to a definitely advanced phased of outward change.'[156]

Conclusion

In this essay, the present author has demonstrated that many accepted "facts" about the history of the Maltese Criminal Code are, in reality, myths, most of which were created because of the dominant ideas which held sway at the time of the Code's drawing

Europe's history to view it as the process whereby, though the agency of Christianity, the northern part of the Roman Empire fused with the "Barbarian" North? But this key is defective, in that it overlooks, and is puzzled by, the later fusion of the now "Barbaro"-Roman (Romanist) civilization with the formerly Muslim South, once again through the agency of Christianity. Whereas the north takes itself seriously (the pagans were really Christianized), it somehow cannot bring itself to believe that really a parallel process took place in the south (and really the Muslims were Christianized). The reason for this could be that this second fusion is more recent than the first one. (This northernmost boundary hypothesis resonates strongly with the 1973 cult movie *The Wicker Man*, the screenplay of which was written by barrister Anthony Shaffer, an English Jew.) Furthermore, using this author's same yardstick, are we to say that the Moroccans and Syrians are "ambivalent Arabs" because they are on the margins of the "Arab world"? But prejudice is bidirectional. The author will never forget when once he was unwell in London and was told by the attending Iraqi doctor that she considers the English "race" dim ... of average intelligence at best! Prejudice is terrible, whichever direction it comes from. When all is said and done, the snow of prejudice should simply melt away under the scorching sun of reason.

155 ASHCROFT, B (2001): *On post-colonial futures: transformations of colonial culture* Continuum International Publishing Group, New York, 36.

156 SAPIR, *op. cit.*, 65.

up and which have been perpetuated because of a lack of historical and self-awareness by later generations. Furthermore, this essay has provided hard evidence that it is incorrect to claim that Scots Law is useful to Maltese Criminal Law on the basis that they share a Roman Law basis.

The present author hopes that a broader result of this analysis is that the Maltese will consider that the key to self-awareness lies in the *forma mentis*. Joining the European Union does mean hoisting the twelve-star blue flag on Malta's public buildings.[157] But it also, and more importantly, means the unfettering of the shackles of at least two centuries of subjection to Orientalism and imperialist ideology. The present author invites the reader to start viewing Maltese (legal) history through Malta's own perspective, building its own "truth".

157 One does not see the EU flag flying on private dwellings in Malta. Till now, only the flags of Malta, the Vatican, the Order of Saint John, and local parish ones, as well as the Marian flag, are flown over private homes. One can drawn one's own conclusions about with what the Maltese homeowner identifies.

Medieval (Legal) Beasts in our Midst? A Terminological *Ad Fontes* Look at the Dissolution of Contracts under Maltese Law

This essay first appeared in *Id-Dritt Law Journal*,
published by Għ.S.L., University of Malta, Vol. 24 (2014).

Medieval (Legal) Beasts in our Midst?
A Terminological *Ad Fontes* Look at the Dissolution of Contracts under Maltese Law

WITH PATRICK A CUIGNET

1. Introduction

ARTICLES 1385, 1438(1) AND (2), AND 1440, and 1419(1) and 1571 of the Civil Code of Malta are examples of provisions which make use of 'dissolution' and '*ħall*' (and/or the relative verbs). However, going back to the origins of these provisions, one finds that the first four (1385, 1438(1) and (2), and 1440) refer to *résolution*. Articles 1419(1) and 1571 refer to *résiliation*.

To compound matters, that same 'dissolution', to which articles 1419(1) and 1571(1) refer, that is, *résiliation*, is then called 'repudiation' in article 1407(1).

These two terms are among many which create difficulties for European lawyers hailing from different jurisdictions.

It seems that the existence of the two French terms *résolution* and *résiliation* has been systematically ignored by other jurisdictions with a Civil Code inspired by the *Code Napoléon*. The Italian (official translation, 1806) and the Latin (official translation, 1806) versions of the *Code Napoléon* (1804) do not distinguish between the two, whereas in the English (George Spence, 1827)[1] translation they were translated erratically. The same erratic pattern can be gleaned from the English versions of the Louisiana (1825) and Québec (1866) Civil Codes.

Maître Patrick A Cuignet studied at the University of Nancy 2, the Centre Européen Universitaire, Nancy, and the Ecole Régionale des Avocats du Grand Est, Strasbourg, France, and has co-authored *Malta at the European Court of Human Rights 1987-2012* (1st edition) with Dr David A. Borg and the present writer.

1 *Code Napoleon, or, The French Civil Code. Literally Translated from the Original and Official Edition*, Published at Paris, in 1804. By a Barrister of the Inner Temple. London: William Benning, Law Bookseller, 1827. Actually the translation is attributed to George Spence – cf. Cushing's *Anonyms: A Dictionary of Revealed Authorship* and Halkett & Laing's *Dictionary of Anonymous and Pseudonymous Literature of Great Britain*.

The Codes of the Kingdom of the Two Sicilies (1819) and of the Kingdom of Italy (1865) follow the Italian version of the *Code Napoléon*. Only the Maltese Civil Code translates them into the consistent though hypernymic *ħall* (with the sole exception of *repudiation – jerġa' lura*).

Is this a mere terminological event which has never been really accounted for? Or have there also been juridical repercussions?

This essay will have an *ad fontes* look at the terminological dimension of these provisions. A future essay might look at the relationship between terminology and the application of the law to investigate whether in this particular case the norms depend on the language used or on the juridical idea behind the written rule.

The relevant articles are quoted in the first two appendices at the end of this essay, along with their analogues in certain other Codes. The articles which in French use *résolution* are in Appendix A; the articles which in French use *résiliation* are in Appendix B. There is a comparative exercise with the French Civil Code (in its French original, Italian and Latin official translations, and English unofficial translation), the Civil Code of the State of Louisiana, the Civil Code of Québec (Bas-Canada), the Code of the Kingdom of the Two Sicilies, and the Civil Code of the Kingdom of Italy. These Codes have been chosen because they have been of direct or indirect inspiration to the Maltese Code. In the case of the Québecois Code, it has been chosen because of the respect it enjoys in comparative law circles as an obtaining bilingual Code functioning in a bijurisdictional legal system.

2. *Résolution* and *résiliation* in French Law[2]

Under French law, *résolution* is the mechanism whereby the creditor of an unexecuted obligation has the faculty to withdraw

2 In its juridically purest form, *rescision* is an action for nullity because of lesion. *Nullité* is the action whereby the contract is brought to naught when it does not satisfy the requisites laid down by the law.

from a contract and bring it retroactively to naught. Unknown in Roman law, this mechanism has its roots in the Canon Law adage that '*fragenti fidem non est fides servanda*'.[3] However, it was not until the 16th and 17th centuries that this mechanism found its practical application, when authors like Dumoulin, followed by Domat and Pothier, demonstrated that *résolution* should apply to all contracts.[4]

Résiliation constitutes another way of terminating the contract which is different from *résolution*. It allows either party to withdraw from the contract without bringing it retroactively to naught. In fact, as the *Vocabulaire Juridique* clearly spells out, *résiliation* is *résolution* in contracts of continuing execution, which obviously are contracts that exclude retroactivity.[5]

Résolution has a wider scope than *résiliation* as it relates to all types of contract. It actually applies to synallagmatic contracts as well as to unilateral contracts such as mandate and pledge, to contracts with instantaneous execution or continuing execution. Whereas *résolution* applies independently of the duration of the contract, *résiliation* applies only to contracts the duration of which is indefinite, and in certain cases to fixed-term contracts, particularly lease[6] and employment contracts.[7]

Both mechanisms can be legal, conventional or judicial in origin. The law provides for the *résiliation* of certain types of contracts (which we shall see below) while article 1184 of the Civil

---

3 English translation: 'One need not keep one's word with those who do not keep theirs'.

4 DOMAT (1822): *Lois civiles, Des engagements* Livre I, tome I, section VI, n°11, t.1 Paris, 301.

5 '*[N]om que prend la résolution dans les contrats successifs qui excluent la rétroactivité*'; CORNU, G (1987): *Vocabulaire juridique* PUF, Paris [the name given to *résolution* of contracts of continuing execution which exclude retroactivity]. *Vide infra* – Barbara Pozzo's thoughts on the translation of these terms in Italian.

6 In virtue of article 15 of the modified law n° 89-462 of 6 July 1989 on the improvement of tenancy relations: '*Le délai de préavis applicable au congé est de trois mois lorsqu'il émane du locataire et de six mois lorsqu'il émane du bailleur*' [The notice period applicable to termination is of three months if notice is given by the tenant and six months if by the lessor].

7 Article L.122-4 *et seq.* of the Labour Code.

Code provides a general power of *résolution* as a condition in synallagmatic contracts. Case-law has come to understand cases of *résiliation* as based on the principle of the prohibition of perpetual commitments to which the Constitutional Council of France has recognised constitutional value.[8]

Résolution is implemented either judicially or else unilaterally in certain exceptional cases contemplated by case-law where the behaviour of one of the parties justifies it.[9] It always punishes the non-execution of a contract and is solidly related to the idea of contractual liability. *Résiliation* is however independent of the idea of punishment ('*indépendante à l'idée de sanction*') and appears more as a reaction mechanism to contractual changes ('*apparaît davantage comme une technique de réaction à l'évolution contractuelle*').[10] It is implemented unilaterally, which is contrary in principle to the spirit of the notion of the contract and provokes the hostility of some authors.[11] *Résiliation* is above all used to protect the party to the contract considered to be the weaker, and consequently it is not perceived in the same terms by the litigants. In the case of *résolution*, the reasoning is different because it is always addressed to the creditor of the unfulfilled obligation and not the debtor.

The major distinction between *résolution* and *résiliation* lies in their respective effects on the contract. Whereas *résolution* brings the contract retroactively to naught, the effects of *résiliation* lie only in the future. In this sense, the effects of *résolution* are close

---

8 Decision of the Constitutional Council of 9 November 1999, RTD civ.2000.109, obs. Mestre.

9 In principle, *résolution* would necessitate judicial intervention. But in certain cases where the fault of one of the parties is serious, courts have allowed the other party to have the contract's *résolution* without judicial intervention. This happened in one particular case, and it seems that French courts have not quite made up their minds on this point.

10 TILLEMAN, B, VERBEKE, AL, VERKINDT, PY (2006): *Droit des contrats* Larcier, Brussels, 183.

11 MALAURIE, P, AYNES, L (1998-1999): *Cours de droit civil, Les obligations* Cujas, n°614, 352; Céline Ruet (1998-1999): *La résiliation unilatérale des contrats à exécution successive* Unpublished thesis, Université Paris XI, Paris n° 172.

to nullity,[12] even though the contract had not been affected by a vice at the moment of perfection.[13] The purpose of *résolution* is thus to put the parties in the same state they were in before, as if the obligation had never existed. If the contract has not been executed, no restitution is due. But in the case of total or partial execution, each party is bound to return what it received. As has already been stated above, in the case of *résiliation* the implications relate only to the future, and, consequently, the party which used the *res* does not give back what has already been executed or used.

According to Boris Starck, contracts of continuing execution cannot be terminated by *résolution* because it is not possible to restore things as they had been before. For instance, the tenant who had been enjoying an apartment for some time, cannot return that enjoyment to the landlord. It follows that in case of non-execution of obligations by one or the other party, the contract cannot be terminated by *résolution* in the strict sense of the word. It can only be terminated by *résiliation*. *Résiliation*, unlike *résolution*, puts an end to the contract with regard to the future but cannot lead to a restitution of what has been irremediably done or acquired.[14]

12 In the case of nullity, a contract is null *ab initio* because of a vice at the moment of perfection. In the case of *résolution*, the contract is null *ab initio* (and in this respect, the effects of *résolution* are exactly the same as nullity) despite the lack of vice at the moment of perfection – the vice appears during the execution of the contract.

13 Certain clauses can still exist despite the retroactive disappearance of the contract, e.g. jurisdiction clauses and sanction clauses, but never non-competition clauses.

14 STARCK, B (1972): *Droit civil* Librairies techniques, Paris, 44. '*Les contrats successifs ne peuvent pas être résolus car on ne peut pas remettre les choses en l'état antérieur, le locataire qui a eu pendant un certain temps la jouissance d'un appartement, par exemple, ne peut pas rendre au bailleur cette jouissance. Il en résulte qu'en cas d'inexécution des obligations de l'une ou de l'autre partie, un contrat ne pourra être résolu, dans le sens exact de ce terme; il sera éventuellement résilié. La résiliation, à la différence de la résolution, met fin au contrat pour l'avenir, mais ne peut pas aboutir à une restitution de ce qui a été irrémédiablement fait o acquis*' [Contracts of continuing execution cannot be the subject of *résolution* on account of the fact that one cannot restore things to their previous state. The tenant who enjoyed a flat, say, for a certain period of time, cannot return that enjoyment to the landlord. It thus follows that in case of non-execution of obligations by one or the other party, a contract may not be subject of *résolution* in the proper sense of the word. It might be subject to *résiliation*, the difference being that *résiliation* puts an end to the contract with regard to the

The solution is not obvious for contracts of continuing execution in which certain obligations cannot be returned in kind. Restitution by monetary equivalence[15] does take into account the value of the thing received or services rendered which cannot be returned. This applies for example in the context of a lease contract when the lessee is not bound to pay the rent but to indemnify the lessor for occupying the tenement. That said, case-law does seem to distinguish between totally-executed and partially-executed or non-executed contracts. In the first hypothesis, only *résiliation* is possible; in the second, *résolution* alone is envisaged.[16]

In the French courts, once the execution of a contract has commenced, then the *résiliation* mechanism is more frequently used, because it would be impossible to return or go back on a past execution. From this point of view, *résiliation* has a practical advantage.

On the other hand, *résolution* has to be pronounced if the execution of the contract has never taken place. Not having executed a contract is a serious fault justifying on its own the *résolution*, in which case *résiliation* presents no practical advantage.

3. The *Code Napoléon* and its Italian and Maltese reception

To borrow HW Harding's words:

> We owe our present Civil Code to the genius of Sir Adrian Dingli who, during his long tenure of office as Crown Advocate, drafted several Ordinances subsequently embodied in Ordinances VII of 1868 and I of 1873. These two Ordinances were mainly based on the Code Napoleon which, in its turn, in many parts had reproduced

---

future but cannot result in the restitution of what has been irremediably done or acquired].

15 'Restitution by monetary equivalence', used by the Québec Civil Code in, e.g., articles 1700 and 1701, is perhaps the best translation of the French concept of *restitution par équivalent*.

16 Court of Civil Cassation, 30 April 2003, JCP 2003, 30, Comment Keira.

> with modifications the principles of Roman Law long established in Malta. These Ordinances were, in certain respects, more progressive than the Code Napoleon because they incorporated provisions containing solutions to the controversies which arose after the promulgation of the Code Napoleon. In drafting these Ordinances Dingli also consulted the provisions of other leading Continental Codes and the treatises of text writers of repute, and did not lose sight of the ancient laws and customs obtaining in Malta as well as the basic principles of Roman Law. He also referred to the Code of Louisiana, itself based on the Code Napoleon.[17]

Among the more important events to take place upon the creation of the Napoleonic Kingdom of Italy in 1805 was the introduction into that Kingdom of the *Code Napoléon*, the *Codice di Napoleone il Grande*, the following year.

Randall Lesaffer writes that:

> In many respects, the *Code Napoléon* of 1804 is a compromise between the ideals of the Enlightenment thinkers and pragmatic realism. It answers to the conservative policies of partial restoration of the Napoleonic regime. It is innovative but nevertheless largely draws on existing law.
>
> It is a mixture of old law and a number of new ideas stemming from the French Revolution. Its 2,281 articles have their roots in customary law, Roman law, canon law, the ordinances of Chancellor Daguesseau and the works of jurists such as Domat and Pothier.[18]

---

17 HARDING, HW (1994): 'Law' in FRENDO, H & FRIGGIERI, O (EDS.), *Malta: Culture and Identity* Ministry of Youth and the Arts, Malta, 216.
Sir Arturo Mercieca wrote that Dingli '*incominciò a studiare seriamente, conscio come era delle sue deficiziene*' only after graduating, going on to become a great statesman, legislator and judge – MERCIECA, A (1954): 'Sir Adriano Dingli: sommo statista, legislatore, magistrato' in *Melita Historica*, Malta: Malta Historical Society 1(1954) 3 164-184.

18 LESAFFER, R (2009): *European Legal History: A cultural and political perspective* Cambridge University Press, Cambridge, 457-458.
To these sources, Pio Caroni adds the Ordonnances of Colbert; CARONI, P (1998): Saggi *sulla Storia della Codificazione* Giuffrè Editore, Milan, 68.

It was traditionally believed that the *Code Napoléon*'s *raison d'être* lay in the ideology of equality, in the sense that everybody in the *Grand Empire* was to be subject to the same law.[19] After all, Napoleon had said that '*ce qui convient aux Français convient à tous*'.[20] Recent scholarship, however, has begun to give due weight to Napoleonic authoritarianism and the Emperor's pragmatic use of civil legislation as *instrumentum regni*,[21] through an '*acculturation plus ou moins forcée des populations*'.[22]

A commission consisting of six (later increased to 10) among the most highly-respected magistrates of the Kingdom[23] translated the Code simultaneously into Italian and Latin. Whereas one can intuitively understand the choice of Italian, the recourse to Latin has still to be clearly explained on the basis of the sources.[24] One could argue that Latin was possibly the only reliable means of spreading the new law in the Italian lands since there it was the language of the written law.[25] At the same time, it appeared that

19 HALPÉRIN, JL (2009): 'A proposito di alcune difficoltà nell'applicazione dei codici napoleonici nei dipartimenti francesi d'Italia' in E Tavilla (ed) *Giuseppe Luosi, giurista italiano ed europeo. Traduzioni, tradizioni e tradimenti della codificazione* Quaderni dell'Archivio Storico, Modena, 265.

20 *Ibid*; English translation: 'What's good for the French is good for all'.

21 *Ibid.*

22 HALPÉRIN, JL (1996): *Histoire des Droits en Europe de 1750 à nos jours* Flammarion, Paris, 61; English translation: 'More or less forced acculturation of the populations'. Halpérin also writes that '*il ne s'agissait pas de remplacer le droit romain en tant que droit supplétif, mais de faire aboutir l'intégration des coutumes et du droit écrit dans une législation commune que la monarchie d'Ancien Régime n'avait pu établir dans le cadre de la société d'ordres. Le Code civil est l'enfant de la Révolution, qui associa la codification au culte de la Loi. Bonaparte est l'héritier de la Révolution, reprenant à son compte le dessein politique de la codification*' [it was not the case of replacing Roman law as supplementary law, but of allowing the integration of customary law and written law within a common legislation which the *Ancien Régime* monarchy had not been able to establish within the framework of the estates of the realm. The Civil Code, engendered by the Revolution, associated codification with the cult of the Law (*loi*). Bonaparte is the heir to the Revolution who made his the political project of codification].

23 DEZZA, E (2000): *Lezioni di Storia della codificazione civile* 2nd ed., Giappichelli Editore, Turin, 97.

24 FERRANTE, R (2011): *Codificazione e cultura giuridica* Giappichelli Editore, Turin, 92.

25 FERRANTE, R (2009): 'Traduzione del codice e tradizione scientifica: la

the Italians' knowledge of French was mostly approximative.[26] In other words, it seems clear that the French strategy was to woo the Italians into accepting the new Code by offering them palliatives in the form of a Latin translation (which then soon fell into disuse)[27] and of the comparisons between institutes derived from French law and the old Roman laws to which the Italians were used.[28] A report drawn up during the prepartory works for the promulgation of the Code speaks clearly of the numerous institutes in the Code which derived from French *droit coutumier* (customary law) and were unknown in Italy.[29]

On 16 January 1806, in Munich, Napoleon signed the Code into force. But before the signing of that decree by the Emperor, there was a brief (almost delusory) moment in which Italian jurists, and the Minister for Justice Giuseppe Luosi in particular, believed that they could create not merely the translation of the *Code Napoléon* but an Italian version of it.[30] Luosi wanted his team[31] to implant a series of exceptions, changes, and additions into the Italian version.[32] He fell prey to Napoleon's charm,[33] to his half-truth that the *Code Civil* was generally based on the Roman laws[34] and to his invitation to adapt the Code to the Italian people's

cultura giuridica italiana davanti al Codice Napoleone' in TAVILLA, E (ED.), *Giuseppe Luosi, giurista italiano ed europeo. Traduzioni, tradizioni e tradimenti della codificazione* Quaderni dell'Archivio Storico, Modena, 225.

26 *Ibid* 227.

27 *Ibid* 237.

28 *Ibid* 232 and 224.

29 DEZZA, E (2000): 'Giuseppe Luosi e il "Codice Napoleone Italiano". Cronaca di una breve illusione' in TAVILLA, E (ED), *Giuseppe Luosi, giurista italiano ed europeo. Traduzioni, tradizioni e tradimenti della codificazione* Quaderni dell'Archivio Storico, Modena, 247.

30 *Ibid* 257.

31 *Ibid* 255.

32 *Ibid* 254.

33 *Ibid* 263.

34 *Ibid* 262. This is described by Dezza in these words: '*mossa magistrale, dal punto di vista psicologico*' [a master stroke from the psychological point of view].

social reality and customs.[35] That dream was dashed by Napoleon himself.[36]

Indeed, the bottom line was that Napoleon ordered a literal translation without adaptations to be completed keeping to a very tight deadline.[37] Before long, both the French and the Latin versions of the Code were eclipsed in Italy by the concordances with Romanistic sources.[38] The Italians could therefore no longer compare the Italian translation with the French original. Not that that would have made their lives easier. Tellingly, in 1864, Federigo Sclopis admitted that the Italian translation had been lacklustre: '*poco esattamente tradotto in italiano*'.[39] One might argue that behind those three words – *poco esattamente tradotto* – hid a number of problems stemming from the inexactitude.

The imprecise translation[40] was further compounded by

35 *Ibid* 260.

36 *Ibid* 261; Dezza's words: '*Tutto svapora e svanisce con il tratto di penna con cui Bonaparte sigla a Monaco di Baviera la traduzione letterale del suo codice con quella sua «griffe illesible» («mais c'était la sienne»!)*' [It all vanished into thin air when with the stroke of his pen Bonaparte initialised in Munich the literal translation of the his Code, with that his '*griffe illesible*' ('*mais c'était la sienne*'!)].

37 *Ibid*; On 5 June 1805 it was established that the translation had to be ready by the following 1 November. The lack of time – or so Napoleon cleverly presented the issue – seemed naturally to lead to the necessity of translating the Code without too much adaptation.

38 FERRANTE (2011) 100.

39 SCLOPIS, F (1864): *Storia della legislazione italiana, III, Dall'epoca della Rivoluzione Francese, 1789 a quella delle riforme italiane, 1847* Unione Tipografica-Editrice, Turin, 159.

40 This phenomenon was not limited to Italy. When, not too long ago, the Government of the Dominican Republic introduced the term *resiliación* to the Civil Law terminology of that country, one local lawyer wrote that in his country they use '*sin mayores miramientos el término rescisión para [to refer] indistintamente a las acciones en resolución, nulidad o resiliación de los contratos*' [with further consideration, the term *rescisión* seems to refer indistinctly to actions of *resolución, nulidad* or *resiliación* of contracts]. This practice, like the Italian one, owes its origins to the translation of their Civil Code from French to Spanish during the 19th century, and the '*mala traducción se impone a los dictados del vocubulario jurídico*' [mistranslation prevails on the dictates of legal vocabulary]; CURY, J: 'Resolución, Rescisión, Resiliación y Nulidad' (Dominican Republic, 2009) <www.jottincury.com/eng/publicaciones/PDF/Civil/CI_09.pdf> (last accessed 3 December 2013).

the alien nature of much of French customary law for the Italians, starkly illustrated by the existence of the said concordances with Romanistic sources (that is, Italian elaborations of Roman Law).[41]

The *Code Napoléon* was soon abolished in practically all those Italian jurisdictions were it had been in force. At the same time, however, it re-emerged as a powerful and almost exclusive model for the civil law codifications which took place in 19th-century Italy.[42]

4. The translation of *résolution* and *résiliation*

Even from a cursory scansion of the articles of the different Codes quoted in the introductory part, it can be concluded that both *résolution* and *résiliation* have been translated into Italian mostly as *scioglimento*. This is the case for the Italian version of the *Code Napoléon*, for the Code of the Kingdom of the Two Sicilies, and for the Code of the Kingdom of Italy. The Maltese Code uses *dissolution* and *ħall* almost throughout.[43]

The English translation of the *Code Napoléon* is quite liberal, using *rescinding*, *annulment*, *disannulling* and *disengagement* as if they were synonyms. The Louisiana Code uses *cancelling*, *dissolution*, *at an end*, and *revocation*. The Québec Code uses *dissolution* and *to vacate*.

But the most telling of all is the Latin translation of the

41 In 1828, an anonymous Italian reviewer of a French legal manual on lease wrote that '*diverse sono in Francia le leggi, diverse le consuetudini, diversi i contratti, diverse le formule, e hannovi persino degli atti pubblici o privati, dei contratti e delle forme di convenzione, che da noi nè pure si conoscono, come il resilimento volontario*' [in France, laws, customs, contracts, formulae, are all different {from ours}, and they even have public or private deeds, contracts and forms of agreement which are completely unknown to us, such as the voluntary *resilimento*] – Anon (1828): *Annali Universali di Agricoltura, Economia Rurale e Domestica Ed Arti e Mestieri*, Vol. 7 Editori degli Annali Universali delle Scienze e dell'Industria, Milan, 125-126; '*Resilimento*', a term which used to be current in Malta as we shall see later on, seems to derive from *résiliement*, which is a variant of *résilation* in French.

42 DEZZA (2000) 103.

43 The original Ordinances are being put aside simply because of space constraints.

Code Napoléon. This was the perfect opportunity for translators to graft onto Italian legal culture the original French notions of *résolution* and *résiliation*. Since the French verb *résilier* derives from the Latin verb *resilire*[44] and *résolution* from *resolutio*,[45] one would have expected to see those two Latin terms used accordingly.[46] Instead, the Italians invariably translated both terms using the Latin *resolutio*.[47] It is necessary to ask whether this was a conscious decision, aimed to disallow the entry into Italian law of any point of French law the doctrinal nature of which was alien to the Italians. Were the Italians resisting the penetration of their legal system by 'barbarian' customs of the North?[48] After all, as the *Dictionnaire d'Étymologie Française* points out, it was only in the Middle Ages that the verb *résilier* underwent a semantic shift, becoming the synonym of *renuntiare*.[49]

A first tentative answer would be in the negative: It was not cultural shielding, at least in this case. It would seem that even in France (and therefore in the original) there was a certain degree

---

44 Disdire in Italian. '*Résilier - mot irrégulièrement formé du L. resilire (salire); pr. sauter en arrière, revenir sur ses pas ; au moy. âge le verbe est devenu synonyme de renuntiare – D. Résiliation*' [*Résilier – a word formed irregularly from the Latin* resilire *(to climb up); to jump backward, to backtrack; in the Middle Ages, the verb became synonymous with* reuntiare]; SCHELER, A (1862): *Dictionnaire d'Étymologie Française* Didot, Paris.

45 *Ibid*; '*Résoudre: L. re-solvere. Du supin resolutum viennent … 2) resolution, fr. résolution, action de dissoudre, cassation, décision, fermeté*'.

46 According to PASINI, J (1814): *Vocabularium Latino-Italicum* Parolari, Venice, 290, Ulpian used '*resolvere emptionem*', meaning '*disfar il contratto*' [undo the contract] and '*ut liceret emptori resilire, meliore conditione oblata*' meaning '*che il compratore, offertagli una migliore condizione, dal contratto ritirarsi potesse*' [the buyer, upon being offered better conditions, could withdraw from the contract]. Furthermore, *resilio*, says Pasini, is defined by Ulpian as '*ritirarsi da un contratto, disdirsi*', whereas *resolutio* is *scioglimento*. But Pasini does not quote a single legal source, quoting instead *resolutio ventris, resolutio nervorum, resolutio stomachi, resolutio sophismatis*. When he mentions Ulpian, as already quoted, Pasini does not say *risolvere il contratto* but *disfar il contratto*.

47 Except in article 1722: *rescindere*, and article 1622: *receder*.

48 Unfortunately, the present authors do not have access to any notes of the Italian translators.

49 SCHELER, *op. cit.*.

of semantic laxity.[50] For example, article 1638 of the French Civil Code[51] speaks of '*résiliation du contrat*'. When discussing this provision in his 1863 commentary on the Code, the French jurist Mourlon uses '*résolution de la vente*' to refer to the same concept.[52] The same lax attitude is encountered in Louis Naz's 1870 essay on the dissolution of sale, for instance in this passage:

> *Il est donc établi que la clause de <u>résolution</u> pour défaut de paiement du prix n'était jamais sous-entendue de par la loi dans la vente romaine ; mais il n'ensuit pas qu'il fut interdit de se soustraire à la rigueur du principe en suppléant au silence du législateur par une réserve expresse de <u>résiliation</u>.*[53]

It is clear that *résolution* and *résiliation* as used here are both referring to the same concept.

As recently as 1924, French civil lawyer Georges Boyer was still speaking of the synonimity between *résolution* and *résiliation* as follows:

> *Plusiers auteurs* [among whom in the footnote the author mentions Baudry-Lacantinerie et Wahl, Louage, I, no. 1391] *ont voulu désigner la résolution non rétroactive des contrats successifs par le terme spécial de résiliation. Leur opinion, admise par quelques arrêts n'a pas prévalu en pratique contre le langage du Code qui parle de résiliation de la vente pour désigner une résolution à effet rétroactif. De nos jours encore, des expressions comme la « résiliation d'un marché »*

---

50 This should not surprise us. Languages are living creatures, in continuous evolution (or degeneration, depending on one's viewpoint).

51 Concordance: article 1419 of the Maltese Civil Code.

52 MOURLON, F (1863): *Répétitions Écrites sur le Troisième Examen du Code Napoléon contenant l'Exposé of sale agreementé des Principes Généraux* A Maresq, Paris, 241.

53 NAZ, L (1870): *Essai sur l'Histoire de la Résolution de la Vente pour défaut de paiement du prix et son état dans le droit français moderne* Durand and Pédone-Lauriel, Paris, 34; English transaltion: 'It is therefore established that a clause contemplating *résolution* because of the non-payment of price was never implied by law in the Roman sale. But it does not follow that it was forbidden to avoid the rigour of the principle by filling in the legislator's silence with an express reservation of *résiliation*'.

> *doivent être entendues dans le sens de résolution. Le langage courant donne même au mot « résiliation » un sens beaucoup plus étendu puisqu'il désigne la dissolution du contrat par* mutuus dissensus *et même par volonté unilatérale dans les contrats comme le louage de choses ou de services* [footnote: *La synonymie des deux mots est antérieure au Code Civil. Dans son* Dictionnaire de droit et de pratique vo. résolution, *Ferrière parle de la résolution du louage pour détérioration de la chose ou non paiement du loyer*].[54]

French law is nowadays more precise in its use of the two terms. Indeed, what Boyer referred to as being still fluid in his day is now the accepted meaning.[55] Italian comparative law expert Barbara Pozzo has felt the need to highlight the inability of contemporary Italian lawyers to find precise terminology to distinguish between *résolution* and *résiliation* in Italian.[56] Professor Pozzo's concern has been echoed by others.[57]

Everything seems to indicate that these concerns are not ill-founded. Italian law dictionaries[58] do not give a precise term as

---

54 BOYER, G (1924): *Recherches Historiques sur la Résolution des Contrats (Origines de l'Article 1184 C. Civ.)* Les Presses Universitaires de France, Paris, 38 [Numerous authors have chosen to use the term *résiliation* to refer to the non-retroactive *résolution* of contracts of continuing execution. Their view, accepted in some court decisions, has not actually prevailed against the language of the Code which speaks of *résiliation de la vente* to denote a retroactive *résolution*. Nowadays, expressions such as '*résolution d'un marché*' have to be understood in the sense of *résolution*. Current language gives the word *résolution* a much wider sense since it denotes the dissolution of a contract by *mutuus dissensus* and also by unilateral will in contracts such as the lease of things or of services. {footnote: The synonymity of the two words predates the Civil Code. In his *Dictionnaire de droit et de pratique vo. résolution,* Ferrière speaks of the *résolution* of a lease on account of the deterioration of the thing or of non-payment of the rent}].

55 *Vide supra* when discussing the current French notions of *résolution* and *résiliation*.

56 POZZO, B (2003): 'Harmonisation of European Contract Law and the Need of Creating a Common Terminology' 6 (2003) *European Review of Private Law* 754, 762-764.

57 *Vide*, e.g., ONUFRIO, M V (2004): 'Harmonisation of European contract law and legal translation: a role for comparative lawyers' in Indret 2(2004) *Revista para el Análisis del Derecho*.

58 E.g., FAVATA, A (2003): *Dizionario dei termini giuridici* La Tribuna, Piacenza, 401-402.

the equivalent to the French *résiliation*. But then, as if it were some terminological legerdemain, a 1994 law dictionary, the *Dizionario Giuridico Italiano-Francese Francese-Italiano*[59] reports the entries *resiliazione* and *resiliare*!

Despite what might have been our initial surprise, it actually seems that this was not the first attempt to transplant these two terms into the Italian lingustic body. For example, the 1842 Italian translation of Pothier's *Opere* carries the phrase '*resiliazione della alienazione*' [*resiliazione* of the alienation].[60] An 1844 collection of domestic and foreign cases published in the Piedmont carries the phrase '*nel caso in questione come una specie di nuovo affittamento verbale, la di cui resiliazione può aver luogo in qualunque anno*' [in this case, it would be like a sort of new verbal lease agreement, the resiliazione of which can take place in whichever year].[61] The 1845 Italian translation of Zachariæ's course on French Civil Law carries the phrase, '*se la perdita avvenne senza colpa del conduttore, questi può riclamare una diminuzione del prezzo, o, secondo le circostanze, la resiliazione della locazione*' [if the loss took place not due to the lessee's fault, then the lessee may ask for a reduction in the price, or, depending on the circumstances, the *resiliazione* of the lease].[62] An 1857 decision of the Genoese Court of Appeal carries the phrase, '*neppure da un tal ritardo possono trarre argomento di consenso alla resiliazione del contratto*' [not even on this late {execution of an obligation} can the argument of the consent to the *resiliazione* of the contract be based].[63] And one other, last,

59 TORTORA, G (1994): *Dizionario Giuridico Italiano-Francese Francese-Italiano* 3rd ed., Giuffrè, Milan, 305, 324, 725.

60 DUPIN SENIORE (1842): *Opere di G.R. Pothier contenenti i trattati del Diritto francese*, Seconda Edizione Italiana, Tomo Secondo Vignozzi, Leghorn, 425.

61 MANTELLI, C (1844): *Giurisprudenza del Codice Civile e delle Altre Leggi dei Regii Stati ossia Collezione Metodica e Progressiva delle Decisioni e Sentenze Pronunciate dai Supremi Magistrati sì dello Stato che stranieri ecc* Luigi Guidetti, Alessandria, 414.

62 ZACHARIÆ, CS (1845): *Corso di Diritto Civile Francese. Prima Traduzione Italiana, Colla Concordanza degli Articoli del Codice Civile per gli Stati di S.M. il Re di Sardegna* Libreria della Minerva Subalpina, Turin, 32.

63 BETTINI, F (1857): *Giurisprudenza degli Stati Sardi. Raccolta Generale Progressiva di Giurisprudenza, Legislazione e Dottrina* Unione Tipografica-Editrice, Turin, 331 (*Loos-Anfossi ed altri*, 17 April 1857).

example: the 1859 *Dizionario Analitico di Diritto e di Economia*, which actually carries the entry *Resiliazione*: '*Italianamente*[64] disdetta, *e rappresenta l'azione in nullità di un atto, ossia la facoltà che la legge accorda a una delle parti contraenti e qualche volta ad entrambe di farsi restituire in intiero, vale a dire di far ritorno alla condizione in che si trovavano prima del contratto*' [In Italian it is *disdetta*, and it represents the action for the nullity of a deed, that is the faculty which the law gives to one of the contracting parties and at times to both to be given a full restitution, that is to return to the condition in which they were before signing the contract].[65] The same dictionary defines *risoluzione* (or *resoluzione*) as '*Atto per virtù del quale si rende come non fosse stato ciò che preesisteva*' [an act which permits the restitution as if what pre-existed has never been].[66] It then refers to provisions analogous to articles 1183 and 1184 of the *Code Napoléon*.[67]

But then it seems that the term merely disappeared, only to reappear in the 1994 dictionary abovecited.

5. *Résiliement*[68] and *résiliment*

An 1808 French-English dictionary, *The New Pocket Dictionary of the French and English Languages*, gives 'cancelling, annulling'

64 One would ask Italian philologists whether this '*Italianamente*' is a clue worth investigating.

65 MELANO DI PORTULA, A (1859): *Dizionario Analitico di Diritto e di Economia Industriale e Commerciale* Giuseppe Cerutti, Turin, 992; Melano di Portula was a *Consigliere di Stato* to the King of Sardinia.

66 *Ibid* 993.

67 *Ibid.*

68 The online etymological dictionary under *résiliation* says: '*Étymol. et Hist. 1429 (Lettre, ap. Lobineau, Hist. de Bretagne, II, 1067 ds Gdf. Compl.); 1740 (Ac.). Dér. de résilier*; suff. -(a)tion*. Cf. anciennement 1611 resiliment « rebondissement »; au fig. « rétraction (d'une promesse) » (Cotgr.), 1624 resiliment « action de résilier » (Cout. de Gorze, VII, 41 ds Nouv. cout. gén., éd. Ch. A. Bourdot de Richebourg, t. 2, p. 1082), 1722 resiliement (Déclaration du Roi du 29 sept. ds Trév. 1743, s.v. resiliation), 1800 resiliment (Boiste)*'; Centre National de Ressources Textuelles et Lexicales <http://www.cnrtl.fr/definition/resiliation> accessed 3 December 2013.

as the equivalent of *résiliation* (*sf.*) and what appears to be its synonym, or quasi-synonym, *résiliement* (*sm.*).[69]

This term, *résiliement*, does not seem to be in current use.[70] However, the *Guide des Notaires et des Employés de l'Enregistrement* of 1803 not only uses it but also defines it: '*Le résiliement est un acte par lequel d'un mutuel consentement on annulle un autre acte pendant que les choses sont encores entieres: ensorte que l'acte résilié est anéanti dans tous ses effets. L'acte qui fait suelement cesser à l'avenir l'effet d'une convention précédente, n'est point un résiliement, c'est une résolution ou une rétrocession*'.[71]

It would seem that the *Code Napoléon* uses neither *résiliement* nor *résiliment*, a term which had been used in the *coûtumes*.[72]

However, early 19th-century Italian texts use the terms *resilimento* and *resilire*. For example, whereas article 1590 of the Italian translation of the *Code Napoléon*[73] lays down '*Se la promessa di vendere è stata fatta mediante caparra, ciascuno dei contraenti è in arbitrio di* ***recedere dal*** *contratto*' [If the promise to sell is made

69 NUGENT, TH (1808): *The New Pocket Dictionary of the French and English Languages* 12th ed., Flint, London, 284.

70 E.g., GUILLIEN, R & VINCENT, J (2003): *Lexique des termes juridiques* Dalloz, Paris, does not carry it.

71 ANON (1803): *Guide des Notaires et des Employés de l'Enregistrement*, Vol. III 2nd ed., Bureau des Instructions Decadaires, Paris, 150. This publication predates the *Code Napoléon*. [*Résiliement* is an act whereby by means of mutual consent one annuls another act while things are still intact. The act subjected to *résiliement* is annulled in all its effects as a consequence. The act which simply halts the effect of a preceding agreement with regard to the future, is not *résiliement*. It is a *résolution* or a *rétrocession*.]

72 For instance, in *Les Coutumes du Pais et Duché d'Angoumois, Aunis et Gouvernement de la Rochelle* (1720), Angouleme: Rezé & Puinesge, 62: '*Et qu'encores aprés cela s'il ne peut payer le prix, dont le vendeur esperoit estre payé contant ... Et defait il n'en est point deu, lors que le Contract est cassé & rescindé ... où il est tenu pour le resiliment*', and in the *Coûtumes Générales du Païs et Duché de Bretagne et Usemens Locaux de la Mesme Province* (1746), Arennes: Guillaume Vatar, 449: '*Reflexions sur ... le resiliment volontaire du contrat*'. ['And even after that, if he cannot pay the price, which the seller hoped to be paid ... And actually it is not due, when the Contract is breached & rescinded ... then it is the case for the *resiliment*'.]

73 *Vide* article 1359 of the Maltese Civil Code: 'recede from', '*terġa*' *lura [minn]*'.

by means of a deposit on account, then each contracting party is free to *recedere* from the contract],[74] an 1811 book meant to carry all the legislation published in the (Napoleonic) Kingdom of Italy from 1802 to 1809 uses the verb we are discussing: '*Se la promessa di vendere è stata fatta mediante caparra, ciascuna delle parti è in arbitrio di* ***resilire dal*** *contratto*'.[75]

An 1834 decision of the *Regia Ruota Fiorentina*, dealing with the question whether a ballerina who marries can disengage herself from her *locatio operis* contract with her impresario because of the change in her marital status, uses the phrase, '*il danno che può risentire un Impresario dal resilimento intempestivo del Contratto legittimamente stipulato con una Virtuosa*'.[76]

Considering the question whether a promise of marriage made in the presence of a State official was to be deemed '*come veri sponsali*', an 1840 Sicilian book on Canon Law taught that '*nel caso che uno de' contraenti voglia resilire ... [la] Legge di Natura [...] comanda che si adempia alla promessa fatta ed accettata, qualunque siasi la sua forma estrinseca*' [in case that one of the contracting parties wants to *resilire* ... natural law ... lays down that the promise made and accepted be adhered to, independently of its external form].[77]

---

74 The French original has used *s'en departir*: '*Si la promesse de vendre a été faite avec des arrhes, chacun des contractans est maître de s'en departir*' ['If the promise to sell has been made with a deposit, each of the contracting parties is free to dispose of it.]

75 *Repertorio Universale della Legislazione pel Regno d'Italia dall'Anno 1802 a tutto l'Anno 1809*, Tomo IV P–R, (1811) Giovanni Parolari, Venice, 255. [If the promise to sell is made by means of a deposit on account, then each contracting party is free to *resilire* from the contract]

76 *Causa Lanari e Rinaldi de Iorca*, decided on 12 April 1834 (Decision XLIII), in CANTINI, L: *Tesoro del Foro Toscano ossia Raccolta delle Decisioni del Supremo Consiglio e delle Regie Ruote Civili delle Prime Appellazioni di Toscana* (1835) Tipografia del Giglio, Florence, 250. [the damage which could be caused to an Impresario by the untimely *resilimento* of the contract legitimately stipulated with a Virtuosa]

77 SALZANO, TMV (1834): *Lezioni di Diritto Canonico Pubblico, e Privato Considerato in Sè Stesso e Secondo l'Attual Polizia del Regno delle Due Sicilie*, Vol. III 2nd ed., Saverio Giordano, Naples, 98.

In his 1853 commentary on the civil law of the Two Sicilies, Annibale Giordano writes as follows on partition:

> *la facoltà di dimandare la divisione è un dritto che risiede in ciascun erede. Una volta questa seguita e perfezionata, non vi è luogo a resilimento, meno che non siavi nell'atto di divisione un difetto di forma o di sostanza, che ne induca la nullità.*[78]

In private correspondence with the present Maltese co-author, Chief Justice *Emeritus* Professor Giuseppe Mifsud Bonnici explained thus:

> *Dan it-terminu jfisser tħassar, tmur lura, allura tikkanċella. L-għerusija u l-konvenju huma l-kuntratti fejn it-terminu l-aktar li jintuża. Naħseb illi s-sostantiv jista' jintuża wkoll fl-appalti fejn in-nuqqas tal-kuntrattur jew anki tal-mittent iwasslu għar-resiliment mill-kuntratt minħabba fin-nuqqas ta' xogħol tajjeb jew ta' ħlas akkont, waqt li jkun għaddej ix-xogħol, mill-mittent.*[79]

In similar correspondence, former European Court of Human Rights Judge Giovanni Bonello explained thus:

> *Riżoluzzjoni, ħall, rexissjoni* etc all refer to legal termination of obligations – either consensually or *officio judicis. Resiliment*, in classic Maltese parlance, was another matter altogether. It was used in two obligations: bethrothal and promises of sale, *r. tal-għarusija, r. mill-konvenju*; these have in common the promise to enter into an obligation in the future. It was thus used in cases of "breach of promise *di fare*", not of breach of an actual obligation. When one of the

78 GIORDANO, A (1858): *Comento [sic] sulle Leggi Civili del Regno delle Due Sicilie*, Vol. III Fibreno, Naples, 217. [the faculty to request a partition is a right which belongs to each heir. Once this is carried out and concluded, there is no possibility for *resilimento*, unless the deed of partition is vitiated in form or substance leading to the deed's nullity.]

79 Emails of the 4 and 17 December 2013. [This term means annulment, withdrawal, and therefore cancellation. Betrothal and the promise of sale are the contracts for which the terms is mostly used. I think that the noun can also be used for contracts of work where the shortcoming of the contractor and also of the employer can bring about the *resiliment* of the contract on account of bad workmanship or of non-payment by the employer while the work is being carried out.]

> parties, unilaterally and against the will of the other party, defaults on the promise to enter into a future obligation (marriage, sale) that act of defaulting is known as *resiliment*. If you see the old judgments on broken promise of marriage, or broken promise of sale, you will find that this 'tort' of the defaulter is referred to as *resiliment*. As to why nobody uses it any more, *desuetudo abrogatoria*. Probably because actions for breach of marriage promise are now very rare, and Italian legal terms are not current with the younger jurists.[80]

The term *resiliment* does not appear in any Maltese dictionary.[81]

6. The implied resolutive condition[82]

Interestingly, a high-calibre author such as Pacifici-Mazzoni, while using *risoluzione* and *scioglimento* interchangeably, is careful to use only *risoluzione* when referring to article 1165 of the (1865)

80 Emails of the 4 and 14 December 2013.

81 *Vide* E Serracino Inglott's and Professor J Aquilina's dictionaries.

82 While there were instances in classic Roman Law when *jurisconsulti* drew certain conclusions on the links between reciprocal obligations if imposed in virtue of the same agreement, they did not perceive the solutions they proposed for particular problems as different applications of the same principle; BOYER, *op. cit.*, 209. There's very little after the fall of the Empire about the notion of dissolution, one solitary example being the Visigoth law on fiefs, whereby free men would forfeit (*commise*) the donations received if they abandoned their *patronus*, a feudal-court-created customary rule later transformed into a juridical construct; BOYER, *op. cit.*, 211. The notion developed later, through Canon Law and the *Coutume de Paris* (especially article 176 and article 177 which deal with the privilege owed to the vendor; BOYER, *op. cit.*, 398 (one can find their text in DU MOLIN, MC (1678): *Coustumes de la Prevosté et Vicomté de Paris* André Soubron, Paris, 281–282. It is pertinent to point out that the northern two-thirds of *Ancien Régime* France were a variegated mosaic of small political subdivisions, each with its very own customary law; that of Paris approximated almost all the others. By customary law we do not mean ancient law which has existed since time immemorial. The *Bibliotheque des Coutumes* (1699) C Berroyer and E Lauriere, Paris, for instance, provides a list of ancient and new customs. Reading them, one feels the text exudes a sense of ease when referring to, and tackling, the obscurity and ambiguity of the law. The fixation, as it were, with precision and clarity was a Humanist and later an Enlightenment priority. In the *Ancien Régime*, lack of precision and clarity was just another one of life's many difficulties which one more or less candidly accepted to live with.

Civil Code.[83] This article is the equivalent of article 1183 and article 1184 of the French Civil Code, and article 1066 and article 1068 of the Maltese Code.

Article 1184 of the *Code Napoléon* reads thus:

> *La condition résolutoire est toujours sous-entendue dans les contrats synallagmatiques, pour le cas où l'une des deux parties ne satisfera point à son engagement.*
>
> *Dans ce cas, le contrat n'est point résolu de plein droit. La partie envers laquelle l'engagement n'a point été exécuté, a le choix ou de forcer l'autre à l'exécution de la convention lorsqu'elle est possible, ou d'en demander la résolution avec dommages et intérêts.*
>
> *La résolution doit être demandée en justice, et il peut être accordé au défendeur un délai selon les circonstances.*[84]

This provision is reproduced in article 1068 of the Maltese Code:

> A resolutive condition is in all cases implied in bilateral agreements in the event of one of the contracting parties failing to fulfil his engagement:
>
> Provided that in any such case, the agreement shall not be dissolved *ipso jure*, and it shall be lawful for the court, according to circumstances, to grant a reasonable time to the defendant, saving any other provision of law relating to contracts of sale.[85]

---

83 PACIFICI-MAZZONI, E (1882): *Codice Civile Commentato con la Legge Romana, le Sentenze dei Dottori e la Giurisprudenza - Trattato della Vendita* Vol. I 2nd ed., Cammelli, Florence, 397, 470. But when he speaks of article 1473, e.g., he uses *scioglimento* (on page 376), and again *scioglimento* when speaking of article 1494 (on page 461).

84 Refer to Appendix C for a linguistic comparison.

85 Maltese version: '*1068. Il-kondizzjoni riżoluttiva tingħadd dejjem bħala li ġiet magħmula fil-kuntratti bilaterali, fil-każ li waħda mill-partijiet tonqos għall-obbligazzjoni tagħha: Iżda, f'dak il-każ, il-kuntratt ma jinħallx ipso jure, u l-qorti tista', skont iċ-ċirkostanzi, tagħti żmien xieraq lill-konvenut, bla ħsara ta' kull disposizzjoni oħra tal-liġi dwar il-kuntratt tal-bejgħ*'.

The implied resolutive condition is found in article 1183 of the *Code Napoléon*:

> *La condition résolutoire est celle qui, lorsqu'elle s'accomplit, opère la révocation de l'obligation, et qui remet les choses au même état que si l'obligation n'avait pas existé.*
>
> *Elle ne suspend point l'exécution de l'obligation ; elle oblige seulement le créancier à restituer ce qu'il a reçu dans le cas où l'événement prévu par la condition arrive,*[86]

and is reproduced in article 1066 of the Maltese Code thus:

> (1) A resolutive condition is that which, on being accomplished, operates the dissolution of the obligation, and replaces things in the same state as though the obligation had never been contracted.
>
> (2) Such condition does not suspend the performance of the obligation, but, if the event provided for by the condition happens, the creditor shall be bound to restore that which he may have received.[87]

It is clear that the combined linguistic effect of these provisions is to legitimate the use of *risoluzione* and *riżoluzzjoni* despite the use of *scioglimento* and *ħall* by the Codes.

7. The Italian position and the Maltese scene

The Italian authors use *risoluzione* and *scioglimento* interchangeably. Not only those of the 19th century, e.g. the Italian translations of

86 The Italian version: '*La condizione resolutiva è quella che, verificandosi produce la revoca dell'obbligazione, e rimette le cose nel medesimo stato come se l'obbligazione non avesse mai avuto luogo. Questa condizione non sospende l'esecuzione della obbligazione; essa obbliga soltanto il creditore a restituire ciò che ha ricevuto, nel caso in cui accada l'evento preveduto con la condizione.*'

87 The Maltese version: '*1066. (1) Il-kondizzjoni riżoluttiva hija dik illi, meta sseħħ, tħoll l-obbligazzjoni, u terġa' tqiegħed il-ħwejjeġ fl-istess stat bħal kieku l-obbligazzjoni ma kienet ġiet qatt magħmula.*

Duranton[88] and Laurent,[89] and Giorgi,[90] but also of the 20th and 21st, such as Torrente-Schlesinger.[91]

The doctrinal situation in Malta is a continuation of the pre-1942 Italian situation.[92] From a terminological point of

---

(2) Din il-kondizzjoni ma twaqqafx l-eżekuzzjoni tal-obbligazzjoni, iżda, jekk il-ġrajja maħsuba fil-kondizzjoni tiġri, il-kreditur ikun obbligat irodd dak li jkun irċieva.'

88 *'Lo scioglimento della vendita'* ['the *scioglimento* of the sale']; DURANTON, A (1848): *Corso di diritto civile secondo il codice francese*, Vol. IX, Titolo VI – *Del contratto di vendita* 2nd ed., Domenico Capasso Libraio-Tipografo-Editore, Naples, 117, para. 374.

89 *'Non dipende dalla volontà delle parti risolvere'* ['Does not depend on the will of the parties to *risolvere*']; LAURENT, F (1882): *Corso elementare di diritto civile*,Vol. XXV. *Estinzione del contratto d'affitto, § III Conseguenze della risoluzione* Naples, 321, para. 375.

90 *'La risoluzione del contratto'* ['The *risoluzione* of the contract']; GIORGI, G (1898): *Teoria delle obbligazioni nel diritto moderno italiano*, Vol. IV – *Delle obbligazioni condizionali, § VII – Della condizione risolutiva tacita* 5th ed., Casa Editrice Libraria Fratelli Camelli, Florence, 214, para. 204. *Vide* GIORGI, Vol. VIII, 304, para. 208.

91 *'Chiedere la risoluzione del contratto, ossia che il contratto venga sciolto e considerato come se non fosse mai stato stipulato'* ['To ask for the *risoluzione* of the contract, that is that the contract be *sciolto* and considered as though it had never been stipulated]; TORRENTE, A & SCHLESINGER, P (2011): *Manuale di diritto privato* 20th ed., Giuffrè, Milan, 645.

92 In the matter of dissolution of contracts, as also in others, the 1942 Italian Code departs from the position of its 1865 predecessor. According to BARGELLI, E (2010): *Il Sinallagma Rovesciato* Giuffrè, Milan, 5, fn. 13, *'A differenza dell'attuale codice civile italiano, il codice francese e quello italiano del 1865, com'è noto, non dedicano un apposito capo alla risoluzione per inadempimento, ma la disciplinano congiuntamente con la condizione risolutiva (definisce l'intero capo della risoluzione del contratto contenuto nel codice del 1942 "una assoluta novità rispetto al sistema del codice del 1865" A. GENTILI,* La risoluzione parziale, *Napoli, 1990, p. 12). Nei codici citati, la risoluzione dei contratti bilaterali viene concepita quale condizione risolutiva sottintesa nel caso in cui una delle parti non adempie la sua obbligazione (artt. 1183-1184 c.c.fr.; article 1165 c.c. it). Si precisa tuttavia che, in tale ipotesi, la condizione risolutiva non opera di diritto, ma presuppone la scelta della parte non adempiente di domandare la risoluzione piuttosto che l'esecuzione del contratto (articolo 1184 comma 2 c.c. fr.)'* [In contrast with the current {1942} Italian Civil Code, the French Code and the 1865 Italian Code, as is well known, do not devote a title dedicated to *risoluzione* for non-execution. Instead, they regulate it together with the resolutive condition (A. GENTILI, in his *La risoluzione parziale*, Naples, 1990, p. 12, says that the new title in the 1942 Code dedicated entirely to the *risoluzione* of contracts is a "complete novelty when compared to the 1865 Code"). In the said Codes, the *risoluzione* of bilateral contracts is conceived as a resolutive condition implied in the

view, whereas the Civil Code uses on an almost exclusive basis 'dissolution' ('*ħall*'), the Courts in the 20th and early 21st centuries have used *xoljiment, ħall* and *riżoluzzjoni* interchangeably.

Passing Maltese cases through the very peculiar sieve we have chosen for the present exercise yields, apart from some interesting and at times unexpected gems,[93] the definite picture that the Maltese follow the Italian pattern, namely using any of the three mentioned terms where the French original had used either *résolution* or *résiliation* as discussed in this essay.

i. **Dr Carlo Moore *vs* Nobbli Dr. Giuseppe Attard Motsito et,** First Hall, Civil Court (Judge Montanaro Gauci), 23 February 1945: – *xoljiment* ipso facto *tal-lokazzjoni*[94] [– the *ipso facto xoljiment* of the lease].

ii. **Antonio Sant *vs* Antonio Mallia,** Court of Appeal (Judges Borg, Ganado, Camilleri), 26 November 1948: – *xjolta u riżolta l-lokazzjoni*; – *riżoluzzjoni u xoljiment tal-lokazzjoni* [– lease is *xjolta* and *riżolta*; – *riżoluzzjoni* and *xoljiment* of the lease].

---

case when one of the parties does not execute its obligations (articles 1183-1184 of the French Civil Code; article 1165 of the Italian Civil Code). However, it must be said that, in such a hypothesis, the resolutive condition does not come into effect *ex lege*, but presupposes a choice made by the breaching party to ask for the *risoluzione* rather than the execution of the contract (article 1184 paragraph 2 of the French Civil Code)].

93 One such gem is the reference to the *Dritt Komuni* by the Court of Appeal (Camilleri, Montanaro Gauci, Harding) in *Anthony Richard Calleja noe v. Joseph Mamo et noe*, 15 December 1952: '*Dan huwa l-applikazzjoni tad-Dritt Komuni; il-ksur ta' kuntratt jista' jikkaġuna dannu, u dana għandu jiġi riparat minn min ikun kiser il-kuntratt, ladarba jkun jirriżulta mill-ineżekuzzjoni tal-obbligazzjonijiet tiegħu*' [This is an application of the *ius commune*; the breach of a contract may cause damage, and this has to be remedied by the breaching party, once the breach results from the non-execution of that party's obligation].

94 This decision refers to a decision of the Court of Florence of the 5 May 1916, *Bencini v Parenti*, which dealt with article 1578 of the Italian Civil Code, a provision similar to article 1324 of our Ordinance VII/1868: '*scioglimento del diritto del contratto di locazione*' ['the *scioglimento* of the right of the lease contract'].

iii. **Vice Admiral Geoffrey Alan Brooke Hawkins *vs* Giovanni Cassar *noe*,** First Hall, Civil Court (Judge Caruana Colombo), 6 October 1952: – *riżoluzzjoni tal-kuntratt* [– *riżoluzzjoni* of the contract] (emphyteusis).

iv. **Anthony Richard Calleja *noe vs* Joseph Mamo *et noe*,** Court of Appeal (Judges Camilleri, Montanaro Gauci, Harding), 15 December 1952: – *riżoluzzjoni tal-bejgħ*; – *riżoluta l-vendita*; – *riżoluzzjoni tal-vendita*; – *riżoluzzjoni tal-kuntratt* [– *riżoluzzjoni* of the sale; – the sale is *riżolta*; – *riżoluzzjoni* of the sale; – *riżoluzzjoni* of the contract].

v. **Amante Gatt *noe vs* Albert Mizzi *noe*,** Commercial Court (Judge Gouder), 31 March 1955: – *riżolut il-bejgħ*; – *riżoluzzjoni tal-bejgħ*; – *riżoluzzjoni tal-vendita* [– the sale is *riżolut*; – *riżoluzzjoni* of the sale; – *riżoluzzjoni* of the sale].

vi. **Rev Kan Don Emmanuele Muscat *vs* Lucy Portelli,** Commercial Court (Judge Gouder), 5 May 1955: – *riżoluzzjoni tal-lokazzjoni*; – *ħall tal-kuntratt* [– *riżoluzzjoni* of the lease; – *ħall* of the contract].

vii. **Emmanuele Falzon *vs* Avukat Dr Joseph A Micallef *et noe*,** First Hall, Civil Court (Judge Magri), 7 May 1955: – *riżoluzzjoni tal-bejgħ* [– *riżoluzzjoni* of the sale]. In this decision one finds a partial exposition of the doctrine on *riżoluzzjoni*, whereby it was held that '*ir-riżoluzzjoni tal-bejgħ iġġib magħha li l-kontraenti għandhom jiġu mqegħda fil-pożizzjoni anterjuri għall-kuntratt, u jirrestitwixxu lil xulxin dak kollu li jkunu rċevew bis-saħħa u in konsegwenza tal-bejgħ. Ir-riżoluzzjoni għandha effett retroattiv, u, kif jinnota Giorgi, 'la sentenza che dichiara risoluto il contratto riconosce uno stato giuridico pre-esistente, e cancellando tutte le conseguenze del contratto opera* ex tunc, *non già* ex nunc, *l'annichilimento del contratto medesimo*' (Obbligazioni, *Vol.*

IX, § 218). Għalhekk kull parti għandha tkun restitwita in pristinum; *għaliex, kif josserva Luigi Mosco fil-Monografija tiegħu* La risoluzione del Contratto per Inadempimento[95] *(paġ. 275), 'il permanere delle prestazioni nel patrimonio degli accipienti risulta sfornito di causa'. U dana r-rifless huwa neċessarjament applikabbli anki għall-venditur, f'każ ta' bejgħ, għaliex anzi, kif jinnota Pacifici Mazzoni, 'il venditore è primieramente tenuto a restituire la parte del prezzo che avesse ricevuto, e che dopo la risoluzione non avrebbe più titolo per ritenere' (*Vendita, *Vol. II, § 31)* ['the *riżoluzzjoni* of the sale has the consequence that the contracting parties are restored to the situation they were in before the contract, and they give back to each other all that they had received in virtue and in consequence of the sale. The *riżoluzzjoni* has a retroactive effect, and, as noted by Giorgi, 'the court decision declaring a contract *risoluto* acknowledges a pre-existent juridical state. By annulling all the consequences of the contract it has an *ex tunc* effect (as opposed to an *ex nunc* effect), namely it extinguishes the contract' (*Obbligazioni,* Vol. IX, § 218). Thus, each party should be restored *in pristinum*; because, as observed by Luigi Mosco in his monograph *La risoluzione del Contratto per Inadempimento* (page 275), 'the continuation of the transferees' financial obligations would no longer have a reason'. This effect is necessarily applicable to the seller too, in the case of sale, because, as noted by Pacifici Mazzoni, 'the seller is first of all bound to give back the part of the price he might have received and which, upon the *risoluzione*, he would no longer be entitled to keep (*Vendita*, Vol. II, § 31)'].

viii. **Charles Santucci *vs* John Mizzi *noe***, Court of Appeal (Judges Mamo, Montanaro Gauci, Harding), 18 May 1959: – *riżoluzzjoni tal-ewwel xiri*; – *riżoluzzjoni ta' bejgħ* [– *riżoluzzjoni* of the first sale; – *riżoluzzjoni* of the sale].

95 MOSCO, L (1950): *La risoluzione del Contratto per Inadempimento* Jovene, Naples.

ix. **Mario Camenzuli *vs* Salvatore Zammit**, First Hall, Civil Court (Judge Xuereb), 16 May 1963: – *riżoluzzjoni tal-lokazzjoni mill-inizju tagħha*; – *ħall tal-kuntratt*; – *jinħall mil-lokazzjoni* [– *riżoluzzjoni* of the lease from its beginning; – *ħall* of the contrat; – *jinħall* from the lease].

x. **Giuseppe Muscat *et vs* Avukat Dottor Tommaso Fenech *et noe***, Commercial Court (Judge Gauci Maistre), 28 November 1963: – *kull kuntratt ta' lokazzjoni jiġi dikjarat xjolt u riżolut* [- every lease contract is declared *xjolt* and *riżolut*]. In this decision, the Court said, '*meta wieħed jitlob ix-xoljiment ikun qiegħed jitlob għall-quddiem u mhux b'effett retroattiv*' [- 'when one asks for the *xoljiment*, he would be making a request for the future, not a request with a retroactive effect']. This is clearly the enunciation of the *résiliation* principle, even though the Court used – like the Italians do – *riżoluzzjoni* and *xoljiment*.

xi. **George Xuereb *vs* Avukat Dottor Edward Fenech Adami *et noe***, First Hall, Civil Court (Judge Magri), 7 December 1963: – *l-attur ikollu dritt ixolji l-konċessjoni subenfitewtika*; – *riżoluzzjoni tal-istess konċessjoni enfitewtika*; – *tiddikjara maħlula b'effett mil-lum il-konċessjoni subenfitewtika temporanea tal-fond* [- the plaintiff would have the right to *ixolji* the subemphyteutical concession; – *riżoluzzjoni* of the same emphyteutical concession; – declares *maħlula* with effect from today the temporary subemphyteutical concession of the tenement].

xii. **Henry Pace *et noe vs* Carmelo Meli**, Commercial Court (Judge Xuereb), 15 May 1964: – *tħoll il-ftehim ta' lokazzjoni* [– *tħoll* the lease agreement].

xiii. **Avukat Dottor Ettore Lucia *noe vs* Avukat Dottor Gaudenzio Borg *et noe***, Commercial Court (Judge Gouder), 6 October 1959: – *il-kuntratt jiġi maħlul*; – *kwindi* *l-attur, li ma għażelx l-eżekuzzjoni tal-kuntratt, imma talab ir-riżoluzzjoni tiegħu* [– the contract is *maħlul*; – thus the plaintiff, who did not opt for the execution of the contract but requested its *riżoluzzjoni*].

xiv. **Remigio Camilleri *vs* Joseph Caruana Soller,** Commercial Court (Judge Caruana Curran), 27 April 1965: – *l-enfitewsi in kwistjoni tinsab risoluta; – risoluzzjoni tal-kuntratt* [– the emphyteusis in question is *risoluta; – risoluzzjoni* of the contract].

xv. **Emmanuele Cutajar *vs* Joseph Grech,** First Hall, Civil Court (Judge Caruana Curran), 10 June 1965: – *riżoluzzjoni tal-kuntratt minħabba inadempiment*; – *riżoluzzjoni per inadempjenza* [– *riżoluzzjoni* of the contract because of non-observance; – *riżoluzzjoni* for non-observance]. This decision carries a powerful review of Maltese cases on the annulment of contracts. It also carries an analysis of the **then** article 1440 (now 1390), an original Maltese provision which does not have any analogous provision in the French or Italian Codes.[96]

96 The Court said that '*jidher li l-leġislatur introduċa l-artikolu 1440, li ma jirrikorrix fil-Kodiċi Ċivili Franċiż jew Taljan, biex sa l-aħħar mument qabel il-konsenja jagħti lill-kumpratur l-opportunità, ġustifikata mid-differenza fil-kwalità promessa, biex jirripudja il-kuntratt ġa perfezzjonat, u joħroġ minnu – jikkanċellah u b'hekk jevita l-inkonvenjenza tal-pagament u tar-riċezzjoni fiżika tal-pagament u r-riskju attendenti l-azzjoni għar-riżoluzzjoni wara li jkun irċieva l-konsenja. [... D]an l-artikolu għandu ċertu vantaġġ ukoll għall-venditur għax meta l-kompratur joħroġ mill-kuntratt qabel il-konsenja, il-venditur jevita l-inkonvenjent u t-telf li jsofri meta jieħu l-ħaġa lura, fi stat użat wara r-riżoluzzjoni*' ['it appears that the legislator introduced article 1440, which does not appear in either the French or the Italian Civil Code, so that up till the last moment before the delivery the buyer is given the opportunity, justified by the difference in the promised quality, to repudiate the already-concluded contract, and withdraw from it – by annulling it and thus avoiding the inconvenience of paying and the physical receipt of the payment, and the risk attendant to the *riżoluzzjoni* suit after the delivery is done. [...] This article has also an advantage of sorts for the seller, since when the buyer withdraws from the contract before delivery is done, the seller avoids the inconvenient and the loss he would suffer if he were to take the thing back upon the *riżoluzzjoni*, when it would by then have been already used'].

xvi. **Emanuele Micallef *vs* Joseph Aquilina**, Commercial Court (Judge Xuereb), 18 June 1965: – *jiġi riżolut in-negozju*; – *riżoluzzjoni tan-negozju*; – *jirrisolvi l-kuntratt*; – *jirrisolvi n-negozju* [- the *negotium* is *riżolut*; – *riżoluzzjoni* of the *negotium*; – *jirrisolvi* the contract; *jirrisolvi* the sale].

xvii. **Accountant General *et vs* Arthur John Ellul Sullivan *noe et***, Court of Appeal (Commercial) (Judges Herrera, Harding, Agius), 14 June 1989: – *appalt jista' jiġi xolt*; – *riżolut il-kuntratt tal-appalt* [– a contract of works may be *xolt*; – the contract of works is *riżolut*].

xviii. **Rosina Grima *vs* Joseph Vella *pro noe et***, Court of Appeal (Judges Said Pullicino, Filletti, Manché), 14 April 1997: – *enfitewsi xolta u estinta*; – *riżoluzzjoni u xoljiment tal-kuntratt ta' lokazzjoni* [– the emphyteusis is *xolta* and *estinta*; – *riżoluzzjoni* and *xoljiment* of the lease contract].

xix. **Albert Sacco *vs* John Camilleri**, First Hall, Civil Court (Judge Sciberras), 31 January 2003: – *riżoluzzjoni tal-kuntratt (appalt)* [– *riżoluzzjoni* of the contract (of works)]. This decision carries an acute analysis of the differences between rescission and dissolution (*riżoluzzjoni*).

It would seem from the above that despite the use of *riżoluzzjoni*, the Maltese Courts – like the Italian authors they base themselves on – are aware that *ex tunc* and *ex nunc* applications of dissolution are intended in different provisions of the Code. This was made explicit in *Giuseppe Muscat et vs. Avukat Dottor Tommaso Fenech et noe.*

This might be the subject for some future essay, which would look into whether the norm contained in a provision depends on the language of the provision or on the intention of the legislator.

8. Conclusion

This essay has examined the passage from one language to another of identical provisions relating to the dissolution of contracts, and how the crossing of linguistic frontiers has caused changes, at least on a lexical level. It has tried to pave the way for a study of any possible semantic shifts caused by the lexical changes. If such shifts have indeed taken place, they should be detected by measuring the application by Italian and Maltese Courts of the same provisions when compared to French doctrine and French judicial practice. Such a study would have to weigh the pros and cons of adopting a diachronic or a synchronic approach.

This essay has also delved into the history of the terms *résolution* and *résiliation*, even going back to their Latin equivalents. A possible conclusion one can draw is that the linguistic confusion which scholars have highlighted owes much to major semantic shifts which took place in the Middle Ages,[97] autonomously and in complete isolation. This might explain what seems to be the resistance by Italian translators to the incorporation of *résiliation* as a term (in its Italianate form *resiliazione*) in their language, which, through a mechanism which would be beyond the scope of this essay to discuss, could then have percolated to Maltese as *reżiljazzjoni*.

Then again, Maltese did accept *resiliment*, even though the dictionaries have failed to record it.

All of this leads to an interesting question about our *Zeitgeist*. One seems to be justified to ask whether *résiliation* is a creature akin to those depicted in that vast book called *Liber Bestiarum* (*Bestiary*)[98] – a Medieval compendium of normal and other animals, improbably-contrived allegorical creatures composed of body parts of diverse beasts, such as unicorns, mermaids, bonnacons and eales, which for our purposes could be taken to represent the hybridisation of Medieval legal knowledge.

97 This is not to say that the later semantic shifts, which have also been discussed in this study, are to be ignored.

98 *Liber Bestiarum*, Manuscript 764 at the Bodleian Library, University of Oxford, United Kingdom.

Despite our Humanist and Enlightenment fixations with order, it seems we have yet to domesticate these medieval beasts.

One possible way of domesticating this particular beast could be by coining the term *reżiljazzjoni* in Maltese and exhuming the defunct short-lived *resiliazione* in Italian.

Post-script

Some time after the first publication of this essay, the Maltese Unit at the European Court of Justice decided to start translating *résiliation* as *xoljiment* and *résolution* as *ħall*. The present author is not privy to the reasoning which lead to such semantic shifts, and can only conclude that the decision was arbitrary, as *ħall* and *xoljiment* are actually synonyms. There is a significant risk that this novelty will lead to even further confusion.

Appendix A
Résolution

EN: ENGLISH
FR: FRENCH
IT: ITALIAN
LAT: LATIN
MT: MALTESE

Article 1385, Kodiċi Ċivili ta' Malta

EN **1385.** If the seller fails to make delivery at the time agreed upon, the buyer may elect either to demand the **dissolution** of the contract or to demand that he be placed in possession of the thing sold, provided the delay has been caused solely by the seller.

> MT ***1385.*** *Jekk il-bejjiegħ jonqos li jagħmel il-kunsinna, fiż-żmien miftiehem, ix-xerrej jista' jitlob, kif jagħżel hu, jew li l-kuntratt jiġi* ***maħlul****, jew li huwa jiġi mqiegħed fil-pussess tal-ħaġa mibjugħa, iżda dan kemm-il darba d-dewmien ikun ġie kkaġunat mill-bejjiegħ biss.*

Code Napoléon

FR ***1610.*** *Si le vendeur manque à faire la délivrance dans le temps convenu entre les parties, l'acquéreur pourra, à son choix, demander la* ***résolution*** *de la vente, ou sa mise en possession, si le retard ne vient que du fait du vendeur.*

> EN **1610.** If the seller fail to make delivery within the time agreed between the parties, the purchaser may at his election demand the **rescinding** of the sale, or to be put into possession, if the delay have occurred entirely through the act of the seller.
>
> IT ***1610.*** *Se il venditore omette di fare la tradizione nel tempo fra le parti convenuto, potrà il compratore chiedere a suo arbitrio o la* ***risoluzione*** *del contratto, o la immissione in possesso della cosa venduta, se il ritardo procede dal fatto del venditore.*
>
> LAT ***1610.*** *Nisi venditor ex suo dumtaxat facto intra statutum tempus rem tradiderit, emptor optionem habebit petendi, vel rei possessionem, vel contractus* ***resolutionem****.*

Codice per lo Regno delle Due Sicilie

IT ***1456.*** *Se il venditore manchi di far la tradizione nel tempo fra le parti convenuto, potrà il compratore chiedere, a suo arbitrio, o la* ***risoluzione*** *del contratto, o che egli sia posto nel possesso della cosa venduta, se il ritardo derivi dal fatto del venditore.*

The Civil Code of Louisiana

FR ***2461.*** *Si le vendeur manque à faire la délivrance dans le temps convenu entre les parties, l'acquéreur pourra, à son choix, demander ou la* **résolution** *de la vente, ou sa mise en possession, si le retard ne vient que du fait du vendeur.*

> **EN 2461.** If the seller fails to make the delivery at the time agreed on between the parties, the buyer will be at liberty to demand, either a **cancelling** of the sale, or his being put in possession, if the delay is occasioned only by the deed of the seller.

Article 1438(1), Kodiċi Ċivili ta' Malta

EN **1438(1).** The seller of an immovable cannot demand the **dissolution** of the sale on the ground that the price has not been paid to him.

> MT ***1438(1).*** *Il-bejjiegħ ta' immobbli ma jistax jitlob* ***il-ħall*** *tal-bejgħ minħabba li ma jkunx ġie lilu mħallas il-prezz.*

Code Napoléon

FR ***1654.*** *Si l'acheteur ne paye pas le prix, le vendeur peut demander la* ***résolution*** *de la vente.*

> EN **1654.** If the purchaser does not pay the price, the seller may demand **annulment** of the contract.
>
> IT ***1654.*** *Se il compratore non paga il prezzo, il venditore può domandare che la vendita venga* ***disciolta.***
>
> LAT ***1654.*** *Si emptor pretium non persolvat, venditor contractus* ***resolutionem*** *petere potest.*

Codice per lo Regno delle Due Sicilie

IT ***1500.*** *Se il compratore non paga il prezzo, il venditore può dimandare che la vendita sia* ***disciolta.***

The Civil Code of Louisiana

FR ***2539.*** *Si l'acheteur ne paie pas le prix, le vendeur peut demander la* ***résolution*** *de la vente.*

> EN **2539.** If the buyer does not pay the price, the seller may sue for the **dissolution** of the sale.

The Civil Code of Québec

FR ***1536.*** *Le vendeur d'un immeuble ne peut demander la* ***résolution*** *de la vente, faute par l'acheteur d'en payer le prix, à moins d'une stipulation spéciale à cet effet.*

> EN **1536.** The seller of an immoveable cannot demand the **dissolution** of the sale by reason of the failure of the buyer to pay the price, unless there is a special stipulation to that effect.

Article 1438(2), Kodiċi Ċivili ta' Malta

EN **1438. (2)** In the case, however, of goods or other movables, the **dissolution** of the sale, even though no express resolutive condition is attached to the contract, shall take place *ipso jure* in favour of the seller, if the buyer previously to the expiration of the time fixed for the delivery of the thing, has not presented himself to take delivery thereof or if on presenting himself to take delivery of the thing he has not concurrently tendered the price, unless a term of credit has been agreed upon for the payment thereof.

> MT *1438. (2) Iżda, meta l-bejgħ hu ta' merkanzija jew ta' ħwejjeġ mobbli oħra,* ***il-ħall*** *tal-bejgħ, għalkemm il-kondizzjoni riżoluttiva ma tkunx ġiet miftiehma espressament, isir ipso jure fl-interess tal-bejjiegħ, jekk ix-xerrej, qabel l-għeluq taż-żmien miftiehem għall-kunsinna tal-ħaġa, ma jmurx biex jirċeviha, inkella, għad li jmur biex jirċeviha, ma joffrix fl-istess ħin il-ħlas tal-prezz, kemm-il darba ma jkunx ġie miftiehem żmien għal dan il-ħlas.*

Code Napoléon

FR *1657. En matière de vente de denrées et effets mobiliers, la* ***résolution*** *de la vente aura lieu de plein droit et sans sommation, au profit du vendeur, après l'expiration du terme convenu pour le retirement.*

> EN **1657.** In the matter of sale of provisions and moveable effects, the **disannulling** of the sale shall take place absolutely and without summons, for the benefit of the purchaser, after the expiration of the term agreed on for taking them away.
>
> IT *1657. Trattandosi di vendita di derrate ed effetti mobiliari lo* ***scioglimento*** *della vendita avrà luogo ipso jure e senza intimazione a vantaggio del venditore, spirato il termine stabilito per riceverne la consegna.*
>
> LAT *1657. Si res annonariae et alia mobilia venierint, ipso jure, et absque ulla interpellatione judiciali* ***resolutio*** *fiet favore venditoris, statim ac tempus ad rem accipiendam constitutum elapsum fuerit.*

Codice per lo Regno delle Due Sicilie

IT *1503. Trattandosi di derrate e di cose mobili, lo* ***scioglimento*** *della vendita avrà luogo ipso jure, e senza intimazione a pro del venditore, spirato il termine stabilito per la tradizione.*

The Civil Code of Louisiana

FR *2542. En matière de vente d'esclaves et d'effets mobiliers, la* ***résolution*** *de la vente aura lieu de plein droit si elle est demandée, sans que le juge puisse accorder de délais que ceux fixés par la loi.*

> EN **2542.** In matters of sale of slaves or moveable effects, the **dissolution** of the sale shall take place of right, if demanded, without its being in the power of the judge to grant any delay, except that fixed by law.

The Civil Code of Québec

FR *1544. Dans la vente de choses mobilières, l'acheteur est tenu de les enlever au temps et au lieu où ils sont livrables. Si le prix n'en a pas été payé, la* ***résolution*** *de la vente a lieu de plein droit en faveur du vendeur, sans qu'il soit besoin d'une poursuite, après l'expiration du terme convenu pour l'enlèvement, et s'il n'y a pas de stipulation à cet égard, après que l'acheteur a été mis en demeure, en la manière protée au titre Des Obligations ...*

> EN **1544.** In the sale of moveable things the buyer is obliged to take them away at the time and place at which they are deliverable. If the price have not been paid the **dissolution** of the sale takes place, in favor of the seller, of right and without the intervention of a suit, after the expiration of the delay agreed upon for taking them away, or if there be no such agreement, after the buyer has been put in default in the manner provided in the title *Of Obligations* ...

Codice Civile del Regno d'Italia

IT *1512. Trattandosi di cose mobili, lo* ***scioglimento*** *della vendita ha luogo di diritto nell'interesse del venditore, ove il compratore ...*

Article 1440, Kodiċi Ċivili ta' Malta

EN **1440.** Independently of the causes of rescission or **dissolution** already mentioned in this Title, and of those which apply to all agreements, a contract of sale may be, in whole or in part, dissolved by the exercise of the right of redemption and may be rescinded on the ground of lesion.

> MT ***1440.*** *Barra mir-raġunijiet ġa msemmijin f'dan it-Titolu, li għalihom jista' jiġi rexxiss jew* ***maħlul*** *kuntratt ta' bejgħ, u minn dawk li jgħoddu għall-kuntratti kollha, il-kuntratt ta' bejgħ jista', kollu jew biċċa minnu, jiġi maħlul bl-eżerċizzju tal-jedd ta' rkupru, u jista' jiġi rexxiss minħabba leżjoni.*

Code Napoléon

FR ***1658.*** *Indépendamment des causes de nullité ou de* ***résolution*** *déjà expliquées dans ce titre, et de celles qui sont communes à toutes les conventions, le contrat de vente peut être résolu par l'exercice de la faculté de rachat et par la vileté du prix.*

> EN **1658.** Independently of the causes of nullity or of **rescinding** already explained in this title, and of those which are common to all agreements, the contract of sale may be rescinded by the exercise of the power of repurchase and by the inconsiderableness of the price.
>
> IT ***1658.*** *Indipendentemente dalle cause di nullità o di* ***scioglimento*** *sopra espresse in questo titolo, e di quelle che sono comuni a tutte le convenzioni, il contratto di vendita può essre sciolto mediante l'uso del diritto di recupera e per la modicità del prezzo.*
>
> LAT ***1658.*** *Praeter hoc titulo enumeratas nullitatis, aut* ***resolutionis*** *causas, et eas, quae omnibus conventionibus communes sunt, venditio, vel jure retractus, vel ob pretii modicitatem revolsi potest.*

Codice per lo Regno delle Due Sicilie

IT ***1504.*** *Indipendentemente dalle cause di nullità o di* ***scioglimento*** *già spiegate in questo titolo, e da quelle che sono comuni a tutte le convenzioni, il contratto di vendita può essere sciolto coll'esercizio del diritto di ricompra, e per la viltà del prezzo.*

The Civil Code of Louisiana

FR ***2544.*** *Outre les causes de nullité ou de* ***résolution*** *déjà expliquées dans ce titre et celles qui sont communes à toutes les conventions, le contrat de vente peut être résolu par l'usage de la faculté de rachat ou de réméré, et par l'effet de la lésion d'outre-moitié.*

> EN **2544.** Besides the causes of nullity or **dissolution** of the sale already mentioned in this title, and those which are common to all

agreements, the contract of sale may be cancelled by the use of the power of redemption, and by the effect of the læsion beyond moiety.

The Civil Code of Québec

FR *1545. Outre les causes de* ***résolution*** *et d'annulation ci-dessus énoncées dans ce titre, et celles qui sont communes aux contrats, le contrat de vente peut être résolu par l'exercice de la faculté de réméré.*

> EN **1545.** Besides the causes of **dissolution** and of nullity already declared in this title, and those which are common to contracts, the contract of sale may be dissolved by the exercise of the right of redemption.

Codice Civile del Regno d'Italia

IT *1514. Indipendentemente dalle cause di nullità e di* ***risoluzione*** *già espresse in questo titolo, e da quelle comuni a tutte le convenzioni, il contratto di vendita può essere risolto coll'esercizio del diritto di riscatto, e può essere rescisso per lesione.*

Appendix B
Résiliation

EN: ENGLISH
FR: FRENCH
IT: ITALIAN
LAT: LATIN
MT: MALTESE

Article 1419(1), Kodiċi Ċivili ta' Malta

EN **1419.** (**1**) Where the tenement sold is subject to non-apparent easements whereof no declaration was made and such easements are of such importance that it may be presumed that the buyer would not have bought the tenement if he had been given notice of them, he may demand either the **dissolution** of the sale or compensation.

> MT *1419. (1) Jekk il-fond mibjugħ ikun suġġett għal servitujiet li ma jidhrux, li tagħhom ma tkunx saret dikjarazzjoni, u dawn is-servitujiet ikunu ta' hekk importanza li wieħed għandu jaħseb illi x-xerrej ma kienx jixtri l-fond li kieku ġie mgħarraf bihom, dan jista'jitlob jew* ***il-ħall*** *tal-bejgħ jew indennizz.*

Code Napoléon

FR ***1638.*** *Si l'héritage vendu se trouve grevé, sans qu'il en ait été fait de déclaration, de servitudes non apparentes, et qu'elles soient de telle importance qu'il y ait lieu de présumer que l'acquéreur n'aurait pas acheté s'il en avait été instruit, il peut demander la* ***résiliation*** *du contrat, si mieux il n'aime se contenter d'une indemnité.*

> EN **1638.** If the estate sold be found to be burthened, a declaration thereof not having been made, with non-apparent servitudes, which shall be of such importance that there is ground for presuming that the purchaser would not have bought it if he had been informed thereof, he may demand to have the contract **rescinded**, unless he shall rather prefer an indemnity.
>
> IT ***1638.*** *Se il fondo venduto si trova aggravato di servitù non apparenti, senza che se ne sia fatta dichiarazione, e siano di tale importanza da far presumere che se il compratore ne fosse stato avvertito, non lo avrebbe comperato, questi potrà domandare lo* ***scioglimento*** *del contratto, quando non prescelga di contentarsi d'un'indennizzazione.*
>
> LAT ***1638.*** *Si fundus venditus servitutibus non apparentibus obnoxius reperiatur, quin de illis in contractu mentio facta sit ; et tanti momenti*

servitutes habeantur, ut emptorem, si id scivisset, rem minime empturum fuisse praesumi possit; is contractus ***resolutionem****, vel pretii indemnitatem pro lubitu petere poterit.*

Codice per lo Regno delle Due Sicilie

IT ***1484.*** *Se il fondo venduto si trovi gravato di servitù non apparenti senza che se ne sia fatta dichiarazione, e queste sieno di tale importanza da far presumere che se il compratore fosse stato avvertito non lo avrebbe comperato, può domandare lo* ***scioglimento*** *del contratto, quando non scelga di contentarsi piuttosto di una indennità.*

The Civil Code of Québec

FR ***1519.*** *Si l'hèritage vendu se trouve grevé, sans qu'il en ait été fait déclaration, de servitudes non apparentes, et qu'elles soient de telle importance qu'il y ait lieu de présumer que l'acheteur n'aurait pas acheté s'il en avait été instruit, il peut demander* ***l'annulation*** *de la vente ou une indemnité à son choix, et dans l'un et l'autre cas, il peut intenter son action aussitôt qu'il est informé de l'existence de la servitude.*

> EN **1519.** If the property sold be charged with a servitude not apparent and not declared, of such importance that it may be presumed the buyer would not have bought, if he had been informed of it, he may **vacate** the sale or claim indemnity, at his option, and in either case may bring his action so soon as he is informed of the existence of the servitude.

Codice Civile del Regno d'Italia

IT ***1494.*** *Se il fondo venduto è gravato di servitù non apparenti, senza che se ne sia fatta dichiarazione, e queste sono di tale entità da far presumere che il compratore, ove ne fosse stato avvertito, non lo avrebbe comprato, egli può domandare lo* ***scioglimento*** *del contratto, quando non prescelga di contentarsi di un'indennità.*

Article 1571(1), Kodiċi Ċivili ta' Malta

EN **1571.** (1) If, during the continuance of the lease, the thing let is totally destroyed by a fortuitous event, the lease is *ipso jure* **dissolved**; if it is destroyed only in part, the lessee may, according to circumstances, demand either an abatement of the rent or the **dissolution** of the contract.

(2) The lessee may also, according to circumstances, demand an abatement of the rent or the **dissolution** of the contract, if owing to a fortuitous event, the thing let has become unserviceable.

> MT *1571. (1) Jekk, matul il-kiri, il-ħaġa mikrija tiġi meqruda għal kollox b'aċċident, il-kiri* ***jinħall*** *ipso jure; jekk ma tiġix meqruda ħlief biċċa minnha biss, il-kerrej jista', skont iċ-ċirkostanzi, jitlob jew it-tnaqqis tal-kera, jew* ***il-ħall*** *tal-kuntratt.*
>
> *(2) Il-kerrej jista' wkoll, skont iċ-ċirkostanzi, jitlob it-tnaqqis tal-kera jew* ***il-ħall*** *tal-kuntratt, jekk, b'aċċident, il-ħaġa mikrija ssir ma tiswiex biex wieħed jinqeda biha.*

Code Napoléon

FR *1722. Si, pendant la durée du bail, la chose louée est détruite en totalité par cas fortuit, le bail est* ***résilié*** *de plein droit ; si elle n'est détruite qu'en partie, le preneur peut, suivant les circonstances, demander ou une diminution du prix, ou la* ***résiliation*** *même du bail. Dans l'un et l'autre cas, il n'y a lieu à aucun dédommagement.*

> EN **1722.** If, during the continuance of the lease, the thing hired is destroyed in entirety by fortuitous events, the lease is **rescinded** absolutely; if it be only in part destroyed, the lessee may, according to circumstances, demand either a diminution of the price, or the **rescinding** of the lease itself. In neither case is there any ground for indemnification.
>
> IT *1722. Se, durante la locazione, la cosa locata venga totalmente distrutta per caso fortuito, il contratto è* ***sciolto*** *ipso jure; se non è distrutta che in parte, il conduttore può, a norma delle circostanze, domandare la diminuzione del prezzo, o lo* ***scioglimento*** *del contratto. In entrami i casi non si fa luogo a veruna indennizzazione.*
>
> LAT *1722. Re locata fortuito, et prorsus percunte, ipso jure contractus* ***expirat****: si pro parte tantum, conductori pro circumstantiis, aut pretii minuendi, aut* ***rescindenti*** *contractus, nulla tamen indemintatis habita ratione, jus datur.*

Codice per lo Regno delle Due Sicilie

IT *1568. Se, durante l'affitto, la cosa locata venga totalmente distrutta per caso fortuito, il contratto è* ***sciolto*** *ipso jure: se è distrutto soltanto in parte, il fittajuolo può, a norma della circostanze, domandare o la diminuzione del* *prezzo, o anche lo* ***scioglimento*** *del contratto. In entrambi i casi non si dà luogo a veruna indennità.*

Civil Code of the State of Louisiana

FR ***2667.*** *Si, pendant la durée du bail, la chose louée est détruite en totalité par cas fortuit ou est prise pour un object d'utilité publique, le bail est* ***résilié*** *de plein droit.*

Si elle n'est détruite qu'en partie, le preneur a le choix de demander ou une diminution de prix ou la ***résiliation*** *du bail. Dans l'un et l'autre cas, il n'y a lieu à aucun dédommagement.*

> **EN 2667.** If, during the lease, the thing be totally destroyed by an unforeseen event, or if it be taken for a purpose of public utility, the lease is **at an end**. If it be only destroybed in part, the lessee may either demand a diminution of the price, or a **revocation** of the lease. In neither case has he any claim for damages.

Civil Code of Québec

FR ***1660.*** *Si, pendant la durée du bail, la chose est entièrement détruite par force majeure ou cas fortuit, ou expropriée pour cause d'utilité publique, le bail est* ***dissous*** *de plein droit. Si la chose n'est détruite ou expropriée qu'en partie, le locataire peut, suivant les les circonstances, obtenir une diminution du loyer ou la* ***résiliation*** *du bail ; mais dans l'un ou l'autre cas, il ne peut réclamer des dommages-intérêts du locateur.*

> **EN 1660.** If, during the lease, the thing be wholly destroyed by irrestitible force, or a fortuitous event, or taken for purposes of public utility, the lease is **dissolved** of course. If the thing be destroyed or taken in part only, the lessee may, according to circumstances, obtain a reduction of the rent or the **dissolution** of the lease; but in either case he has no claim for damages against the lessor.

Codice del Regno d'Italia

IT ***1578.*** *Se durante la locazione la cosa locata è totalmente distrutta, il contratto è* ***sciolto*** *di diritto: se non è distrutta che in parte, il conduttore può secondo le circostanze domandare la diminuzione del prezzo o lo* ***scioglimento*** *del contratto. In ambidue i casi non si fu luogo a veruna indennità, se la cosa è perita per caso fortuito.*

Article 1407(1), Kodiċi Ċivili ta' Malta

EN **1407. (1)** The action of the seller for an increase of the price, and the action of the buyer for a diminution of the price or for **repudiation** of the contract shall be barred by the lapse of two years from the day of the contract.

> MT *1407. (1) L-azzjoni li tmiss lill-bejjiegħ għaż-żjieda tal-prezz, u dik li tmiss lix-xerrej għat-tnaqqis tal-prezz jew biex* ***jerġa' lura*** *mill-kuntratt, tintilef għeluq sentejn minn dak in-nhar tal-kuntratt.*

Code Napoléon

FR *1622. L'action en supplément de prix de la part du vendeur, et celle en diminution de prix ou en* ***résiliation*** *du contrat de la part de l'acquéreur, doivent être intentées dans l'année, à compter du jour du contrat, à peine de déchéance.*

> EN **1622.** The action for addition to the price on the part of the seller and that for diminution of price or that for **disengagement** from the contract on the part of the purchaser, must be brought within a year, computing from the day of the contract, on pain of non-suit.
>
> IT *1622. L'azione pel supplimento del prezzo, che compete al venditore, e quella per la diminuzione del prezzo o per il* ***recesso*** *del contratto che compete al compratore, devono proporsi entro un anno, da computarsi dal giorno del contratto, sotto pena della perdita delle loro ragioni.*
>
> LAT *1622. Actiones ad pretii suplementum consequendum, quae venditori, et ad pretii deminutionem, vel ad* ***recedendum*** *a contractu, quae emptori competunt, intra annum a die contractus instituendae sunt, que elapso extinguuntur.*

Codice per lo Regno delle Due Sicilie

IT *1468. L'azione pel supplimento del prezzo, che compete al venditore, e quella per la diminuzione del prezzo, o pel* ***recesso*** *dal contratto, che compete al compratore, debbono proporsi entro un anno da computarsi dal giorno del contratto, sotto pena della perdita delle loro ragioni.*

Civil Code of Louisiana

FR *2474. L'action en supplément de prix et celle en diminution de prix ou en* ***résiliation*** *du contrat de la part de l'acquéreur, doivent être intentées dans l'année, à compter du jour du contrat, à peine de déchéance.*

> EN **2474.** The action for supplement of the price on the part of the seller, and that for diminution of the price, or for the **cancelling** of the contract on the part of the buyer, must be brought within one year from the day of the contract, otherwise it is barred.
>
> EN **2498.** The seller's action for an increase of the price and the buyer's actions for diminution of the price or **dissolution** of the sale

for shortage or excessive surplus in the extent of the immovable sold prescribe one year from the day of the sale.

Civil Code of Québec

FR *1504. L'action en supplément de prix, de la part du vendeur, et celle en diminution de prix, ou en* ***rescision*** *du contrat, de la part de l'acheteur, sont sujettes aux règles générales de la prescription.*

EN **1504.** The action for supplement of price on the part of the seller, or for diminution of price, or for **vacating** the contract, on the part of the buyer, is subject to the general rules of prescription.

Codice del Regno d'Italia

IT *1478. Nei casi sopra espressi l'azione pel supplemento del prezzo che spetta al venditore, e quella per diminuzione del prezzo o pel* ***recesso*** *dal contratto che spetta al compratore, debbono proporsi nel termine di un anno dal giorno del contratto, sotto pena della perdita delle rispettive ragioni.*

Appendix C

In George Spence's English translation of the *Code Napoléon*, article 1184 reads as follows:

> A condition dissolutory is always intended in synallagmatical contracts, for the case in which one of the two parties shall not satisfy his engagement.
>
> In this case the contract is not dissolved absolutely. The party towards whom the engagement has not been performed, has his election either to compel the other to performance of the agreement where it is promise of sale agreementsible, or to demand the dissolution thereof with damages and interest.
>
> The dissolution may be demanded at law, and a delay may be granted to the defendant according to circumstances.

Ironically enough, it would seem that the Civil Code of Québec does not carry an analogous provision.

The Code of the Kingdom of the Two Sicilies carries a verbatim translation in article 1137:

> *La condizione risolutiva è sempre sottintesa ne' contratti sinallagmatici, nel caso che una delle parti non soddisfaccia alla sua obbligazione. In tal caso il contratto non è sciolto ipso jure. La parte verso cui non si è eseguita l'obbligazione, ha la scelta o di costringere l'altra all'adempimento della convenzione, essendo ciò possibile, o di dimandare lo scioglimento insieme co' danni ed interessi.*

The Civil Code of Louisiana too carries the same provision, in article 2041:

> *La condition résolutoire est toujours sous-entendue dans tous les contrats commutatifs, pour le cas où l'une des deux parties ne satisferait point à ses engagemens : dans ce cas, le contrat n'est pas nul de plein droit; la partie qui se plaint de la violation du contrat peut ou demander sa résolution avec dommages-intérêts, ou son exécution si elle est possible.*

> A resolutory condition is implied in all commutative contracts, to take effect, in case either of the parties do not comply with his engagements: in this case the contract is not dissolved of right; the party complaining of a breach of the contract may either sue for its dissolution, with damages, or, if the circumstances of the case permit, demand a specific performance.

And in article 2042:

> *Dans tous les cas, the résolution d'un contrat peut être demandée par action ou par voie d'exception; et lorsque la condition résolutoire repose sur un évènement qui ne dépend pas de la volonté de l'une ou de l'autre des parties, le contract est résolu de plein droit ; mais dans les autres cas elle doit être demandée en justice, et la partie qui se trouve en défaut peut, suivant les circonstances, obtenir un délai pour exécuter la condition.*

> In all cases, the dissolution of a contract may be demanded by suit or by exception, and when the resolutory condition is an event, not depending on the will of either party, the contract is dissolved of right, but, in other cases, it must be sued for; and the party in default may, according to circumstances, have a further time allowed for the performance of the condition.

The Civil Code of the Kingdom of Italy does likewise, in article 1165:

> *La condizione risolutiva è sempre sottintesa nei contratti bilaterali, pel caso in cui una delle parti non soddisfaccia alla sua obbligazione. In questo caso, il contratto non è sciolto di diritto. La parte, verso cui non fu eseguita l'obbligazione, ha la scelta, o di costringere l'altra all'adempimento del contratto, quando sia promise of sale agreementsibile, o di domandare lo scioglimento, oltre il risarcimento dei danni in ambedue i casi. La risoluzione del contratto deve domandarsi giudizialmente, e può essere concessa al convenuto una dilazione secondo le circostanze.*

Latin Wine Decanted into a Semitic Carafe: The Obscure Term "*Midheb*" in Vassalli's *Lexicon* and its Possible Usefulness for the Legal Historian

This essay first appeared in *Melita Historica*,
published by the Malta Historical Society, Vol. 16 No. 1 (2012).

Latin Wine Decanted into a Semitic Carafe: The Obscure Term "*Midheb*" in Vassalli's *Lexicon* and its Possible Usefulness for the Legal Historian

> 'European fears of Islam actually stem from a history of similarity. [...]
> Few societies illustrate [this] as strikingly as Malta.
> Its language and urbane modern history, circling ports,
> argue for the idea of culture as fusion'.
> – Ranier Fsadni[1]

Preamble

THE PRESENT AUTHOR thinks it his duty to make two declarations by way of introduction. First, he is not a professional linguist, and secondly, his knowledge of legal history is limited to *internal* Western European legal history. Thus, whereas it is implicit in every research that conclusions are valid until proved wronged, the author would like to underline that the conclusions in this essay, being speculative in nature, are explicitly subject to the hope that future specialist research and discoveries (possibly of documents) will confirm or confute them. The author feels very much like someone who is snorkelling, sees some ancient relic on the bottom of the sea and tells the others about it, hoping someone better equipped manages to dive down and have a closer, better look.

In this essay, the author will report about an obscure term he has found, and discuss his understanding of it.

Premise

In the *Lexicon*[2] of Mikiel Anton Vassalli (1764-1829, a national hero of Malta, considered the Father of the Maltese Language),

---

The author acknowledges that he borrowed the metaphor used in the title from Guido de Marco (1931 2010) who used it in 1997 during the post-prandial conversation when the author's father invited the future President of Malta to dinner at their home.

1 "Did Breivik have a point?" in *The Times* (Malta 28 July 2011) 8.

2 VASSALLI, M A (1796/2002): *Ktŷb yl Klŷm Mâlti 'Mfysser Byl-Latĭn u Byt-Taljân* Rome; SKS, Malta.

under the letter "M", one finds a very curious entry: *midheb*. After cross-referencing to *din*,[3] Vassalli defines *midheb* as "*Lex propria & privata*, hinc *Lex & usus nationis, ritus*". Vassalli limits the definition to Latin, omitting Italian – probably a wise decision in this case.[4]

At least two late 20th-century dictionaries have reproposed Vassalli's entry, but there seems to be a general inability to understand its real meaning, also because it would seem that the term has been in disuse for a very long time.

Many questions arise from this entry, the two most urgent of which regard: (i) its meaning and (ii) the possibility of the existence of a non-Italianate Maltese legal terminology at the end of the 18th century, or at least a lingering memory of it. This essay will try to answer both.

1. Introduction

'*Midheb*' does not feature in Giovanni Battista Falzon's *Dizionario maltese-italiano-inglese* (1845), and neither in Giuseppe Maria Barbera's *Dizionario maltese-arabo-italiano* (1939)[5] nor in Mario Serracino-Inglott's *Id-Dizzjunarju Malti u Teżawru ta' Malti mħaddem* (2000).[6] But it *is* reproduced by Erin Serracino Inglott

---

3 'Mydheb, m.s., mdŷhĕb pl. = Dĭn V.'

4 Vassalli (*op. cit.*, XXXVIII) says generally, '*Ad alcuni [...] vocaboli detti la significazione in una sol lingua, quando questa combinava in tutte due; e ciò per non dilungare l'argomento*' ['I have explained some entries in only one language, when it was possible to combine both languages in one; and this I did so as not to dwell on the argument'].

5 I am omitting Vincenzo Azopardi's (1856/2009) *Piccolo Dizionario* Għaqda tal-Malti – Università, Malta, and Thesan's (c. 1600/1999) *Maltese-Italian dictionary* Mons. Lawrenz Cachia, Malta, on purpose, since neither features the entry anyway – a fact which, of itself, has very little consequence in view of the limited number of words each dictionary carries.

6 The word does not appear in Girolamo Caracausi's (1930) *Arabismi Medievali di Sicilia* Centro di Studi Filologici e Linguistici Siciliani, Palermo, either. Also, Vassalli (1828/2006) registers no proverb with the word *midheb* in his *Motti, Aforismi e Proverbii maltesi*, Argo, Malta. Godfrey Wettinger (2006) does not mention it in his *Kliem Malti Qadim* Istitut tal-Lingwistika, Università ta' Malta, Malta, and neither does Stanley Fiorini (1999) in his "Ut Vulgo Dicitur: Pre-1600 Materials

(ESI) in his *Il-Miklem Malti* (1977) and by Ġużè Aquilina in his *Maltese-English Dictionary* (1990).

ESI carries *verbatim*, and then translates, Vassalli's definition of *midheb*, but adds two elements which are not found in the original. Of significance is his report that his attempts to find out whether Vassalli's definition was still current proved fruitless inducing him to conclude – logically – that the term had fallen in disuse.

Aquilina, on the other hand, tells us: "**midheb** [Vass]. **1.** A large quantity of gold. **2.** Established opinion/habit/custom of a people. See *deheb*."

1.1 Nothing to do with gold, in whichever quantity

Let us consider Aquilina's first definition, relating to *gold* (*deheb*), as the possible origin of the term *midheb*. Vassalli does *not* give "a large quantity of gold" as one of the definitions of *midheb*. It is indeed ESI who defines it thus, presumably because that is what he was told in Birgu.[7] Aquilina must have followed ESI even though the absence of *mifded* or *maħded* (from *fidda* - silver, and *ħadid* - iron, respectively) should have sounded the alarm bells. It might also have been the case that ESI was misled by *maħtab*: '*quantità grande o catasta di legno*' ['large quantity or a stack of wood'] and *mixbek*: '*quantità di reti*' ['quantity of nets'] (even though Vassalli does not define all such nouns as denoting large quantities).

It would therefore seem that both ESI and Aquilina err when suggesting the connection with *deheb* (gold). Indeed, the term *midheb* has another root, even though with the same three consonants like *deheb*: ذ (*dhaal*), ه (*haa'*) and ب (*baa'*); however, *midheb*'s root is not related to *gold*, because – and here's the twist – its root is not used in Maltese. It is D-Ħ-B, whence the Arabic

for a Documented Etymology of Maltese" in *Karissime Gotifride: Historical essays presented to Godfrey Wettinger on his seventieth birthday*, Paul Xuereb ed., Malta University Press, 161-177. Moreover, the word does not appear in Agius Sultana's *Damma*, reissued in 2016 (edited by Rosabelle Carabott).

7 "*Ħadd aktar ma jagħti l-kelma, anqas fit-tifs. ewlieni li smajt jingħad il-Birgu!*" - ["Nobody else enumerates this term, not even in the principal meaning I've heard in Birgu!"] – *Il-Miklem Malti* (1979) Klabb Kotba Maltin, Malta, Vol. VI, 131.

verb "to go" (*dhahab*).[8] Vassalli does not enumerate *daħab* (or *dahab*) as a verb, not even as an *obsoletum* as he does with other verbs (e.g., *daħan*).

Whereas the Arabic *dheheb* (*gold*) shares the same root with the Hebrew word for *gold*, namely *zahav*,[9] the word *midheb* - which ultimately derives from the Arabic verb *dh-h-b*, "to go" - is equivalent to the Hebrew word *halakhah*, which similarly derives from the Hebrew verb "to go", *h-l-kh*. Indeed, it has been argued that the Arabic term (*madhhab* = *midheb*) goes back to the Hebrew term *halakhah*.[10]

Since they are here referring exactly to the same concept, and the Hebrew word has no connection with the word for *gold*, it would seem clear that *midheb* does not refer to large quantities of gold.

1.2 It is a legal term

Indeed Aquilina mistranslates the definition Vassalli gives us in Latin. Aquilina translates as "established opinion/habit/custom of a people" what ESI reports as "*mġiba, fehma ta' ġens li, biż-żmien, issir drawwa, użanza, liġi; din; opinjoni ġenerali*". Both work on

---

8 The *Al-Mawrid Arabic-English Dictionary* (2005) Dar El-Ilm Lilmalayin, Beirut, gives "faith, belief, creed; doctrine, teaching, ideology; school; (orthodox) rite" for مذهب [madhhab]. Interestingly, the next term is مذهّب [madhhhab] the meaning of which is not a "large quantity of gold" but "gilded", "gilt". Though there might be some justification in arguing that one should look up the term in 18th century Arabic dictionaries in order better to understand Vassalli's term, it would seem - as will be shown later - that the term مذهب did not undergo semantic shifts.

9 *Dhaal*, *haa'* and *baa'* in Arabic are equivalent to *zayin*, *he'* and *beyth* in Hebrew.

10 LAZARUS-YAFEH, H (1979): 'Judeo-Arabic culture' in ROTH C. (ED.) *Encyclopaedia Judaica Yearbook 1977/78* Keter Publishing House Ltd, Jerusalem, 105. As a matter of fact, 'influences of Talmudic on Ancient Islamic law [...] have often been pointed out and are easy to account for' - SCHACHT, J (1950): "Foreign Elements in Ancient Islamic Law", *Journal of Comparative Legislation and International Law*, Third Series, Vol. 32, No. 3/4 (Cambridge University Press on behalf of the British Institute of International and Comparative Law, Cambridge 1950) 10. As recently as 2005 it has been argued that the legal contents of the *Quran* may be 'viewed in the larger context of already established Jewish law and the ancient Semitic-Mesopotamian legal traditions' - HALLAQ, WB (2005): *Origins and Evolution of Islamic Law* Cambridge University Press, Cambridge, 4.

and misconstrue Vassalli's original: "*lex propria & privata;* hinc: *lex & usus nationis: ritus*".

Despite the cautious approach to the translation, we can note that ESI added *opinjoni ġenerali* to Vassalli's definition. Probably ESI was influenced by what he found in Arabic dictionaries, "*opinion en général, non seulement quand il s'agit de la religion*". But this addition is extraneous to Vassalli's succinct and precise definition: *lex propria* and *lex privata*, hence the *law and the custom of a people*[11]*: rite.*

ESI is however faithful to Vassalli by translating *ritus* as *din*, which, Vassalli tells us, means, apart from conscience[12] and religion,[13] '*animi proprietas vel habitus, mos, ritus, consuetudo – inclinazione naturale, naturalezza, modo e proprietà d'oprare*'. ESI tries to convey Vassalli's meaning by adding *drawwa* which Vassalli had defined also as *usus, mos, consuetudo*. Not being a 'man of law', ESI must have felt frustrated groping in the dark.[14]

---

11 This is still the pre-Romantic stage in European thought, and *natio* is still not "nation" but more or less "people". (The Maltese for *natio* is *tajfa*; *tajfet il-Maltin* = *natio vel gens Melitensium, nazione Maltese* [Maltese nation].) Vassalli lived at that historical moment when the Enlightenment outlook left rationalism and moved toward the romantic revolt. As an aside, Frans Sammut's novel *Il-Ħolma Maltija* is based on precisely this movement: Part I is the 'Rationalist' awakening; Part II the result of that rationalist awakening; Part III the 'Romantic' development which Vassalli achieves through his political involvement instigated by the Secret Society. To the present author, it is evident that the novel's structure mirrors a Masonic temple: between the two pillars (Part I and Part III) lie the implements, the compass and the square holding a "G" or the all-seeing eye (the desire to identify the individual conscience with the will of God) in the middle (Part II).

12 *Coscienza, conoscimento delle operazioni.*

13 *Religione, culto.*

14 Probably the same can be said about Corriente's definition of *maδhab* as *opinion, belief* (*vide* CORRIENTE, F (1997): *A Dictionary of Andalusi Arabic*, Brill, The Netherlands). Non-technical, general-purpose dictionaries cannot go beyond scratching the surface; in this case, they accept opinion and belief without delving further – they leave that task to specialist dictionaries, and rightly so. (It is interesting to note that Corriente gives the word with a "*h*" (Maltese *h*) rather than a "*ḥ*" (Maltese *ħ*), which would seem to imply the same pronunciation as in Maltese.) – I must here acknowledge my indebtedness toward my late father for the intuition to look at Al-Andalus Arabic for a branch of Arabic closer to Maltese, if not its direct progenitor – SAMMUT, F (2009): *Introduction to Azopardi's Piccolo Dizionario* Għaqda tal-Malti – Università, Malta, *passim*.

2. The meaning of the term

From here onwards, we shall adopt a two-pronged approach. We shall look at the Semitic origins of *midheb*, and its meaning in the Semitic world, and then at the Romanist meaning which one assumes the same word to have acquired in Malta.

We shall look at Islamic and Jewish legal systems, albeit in a cursory fashion, in order to understand the meaning of the term.

We shall then look at the *Ancien Régime* system in Europe[15] to which Vassalli was certainly referring.[16] The implicit premise here obviously is that the Muslim, the Jewish and the European legal traditions are different from each other, despite similarities and cross-fertilisations.[17]

2.1 The Arabic word *madhhab*

The etymological origins of *midheb*, as we have already said, lie in the Arabic word *madhhab* (which is equivalent to the Jewish word *halakhah*, about which later).

Madhhab derives from the verb which literally means "to go".[18] *Midheb*, or *madhhab* in Arabic, is a verbal noun meaning "that which is followed and, more specifically, the opinion or idea that one chooses to adopt".[19]

It is a "school of law", by which we mean a body of doctrinal legal opinions, rather than a place where law is taught,[20] which

---

15 By which, broadly speaking, we mean Western Europe before 1789.

16 Is it safe not to assume that it is highly improbable that the Maltese already had a word in the vernacular for the nascent legal ideas of the time?

17 *Vide* PATRICK GLENN, H (2010): *Legal Traditions of the World* (4th ed.), Oxford University Press, Oxford, for a more detailed analysis.

18 HALLAQ, W (2005): *The Origins and Evolution of Islamic Law* Cambridge University Press, Cambridge, 150.

19 *Ibid.*

20 We know from the biographies of some Sicilian scholars that advanced studies in Islamic law in Sicily were taught at institutions (mosque-schools) which in the 11th century became known as *madrasahs* (CHIARELLI, L (2010): *A History of Muslim Sicily* Midsea Books, Malta, 296). Is it reasonable to presume that there was no *madrasah* in Malta, but that there was *madhhab*? DE BONO, P (1897): *Sommario*

would be a *madrasah.*[21]

---

della Storia della Legislazione in Malta Tipografia del Malta, Valletta, makes no mention of law schools in Malta during Arab times. I quote a dated book because there is no other literature, to my knowledge, which deals with law during Malta's Arab period.

21 Interestingly, Vassalli does not register the term *madrasa* (or anything similar – instead he gives *dar il-għerf* for *scuola* and *dar it-tagħlim* for *seminario*) in his *Lexicon.* Before the skeptic rises to his feet to insinuate that there goes a purist set on coining phrases, there are other terms: *dar ix-xjaten* (*inferno*), *dar is-sliema* (*paradiso* – Vassalli gives this as *ġenna*'s second meaning, the first being an enclosure replete with trees and delights), *dar ir-rħib* (*abitazione de' frati*) and *dar il-bniet* (*monistero delle femmine*) which, to put the sceptic's mind at rest, survives as the title of a noble family. On the other hand, we have to take note of the fact that Vassalli was 'very critical of the indiscriminate acceptance of loans and considers the city dialect as "*il più corrotto*" ("the most corrupt") both for this reason and for the extensive code-mixing which was practised in this area' – MIFSUD, M (1995): *Loan Verbs in Maltese: A Descriptive and Comparative Study* Brill, The Netherlands, 1. This might explain why Vassalli qualifies '*ċens*' (*enfiteusi, livello*) in his dictionary (Thesan gives it too) as a *vox non orientalis*, a barbarism that is, and then gives us *qanûn* (different from *qanŭn*, "*canone, regola*") as the equivalent of *canone, livello*, meaning a ground rent, that is to say the payment made by an inferior owner to the superior owner of the same land in recognition of the "latent" rights of the latter on the land. (It would be beyond the scope of the present essay to go into the institute of emphyteusis, that exquisite Medieval creation of the Italian notaries, who moulded the Roman Law of Antiquity to suit their immediate socio-economic needs – see Paolo Grossi's (1995) *L'Ordine Giuridico Medievale*, Laterza, Bari-Rome, for an exhaustive analysis. At the same time, it is worth recording that RICHERI, TM (1792): *Dictionarium Juris Civilis, Canonici et Feudalis nec non delectus legum feudalium* Turin, Ex Typographia regia defines *census* as '*census hodie dicitur contractus, quo quis pretio accepto alteri vendit jus percipiendi annuam pensionem ex re fructifera…*'. Vassalli's parsimony with *voces non orientales* could also explain the absence of terms such as *avukat* and *nutar*. For *nutar*, Vassalli gives *kyttŷb* but he also uses that term for other "people who write", not just the notary. When writing his novel *Il-Ħolma Maltija*, Vassalli's fictional autobiography, Frans Sammut had to make use of *avukat* for the (historically real) character Giuseppe Elia Pace, who had been a friend of Vassalli's and a Minister during the Jacobin Republic of Rome the reason being that there is no *vox orientalis* for *advocatus / avvocato* in the Lexicon. But *nutar* and *avukat* do appear in Falzon's 1845 *Dizionario Maltese-Italiano-Inglese*, along with what today we would write as *leġiżlattiv*. Likewise, Vassalli does not give *liġi*, and neither *qorti*, but he does define *ħaqq* as, *inter alia*, *jus* and *tribunal*, *forum* (he even quotes '*Il-ħaqq tal-Imdina, tal-Belt*') and *manbar* as *tribunale*. But about this, later.

2.2.1 *Madhhab* in Islamic Law

The sources of Islamic law are the *Quran* and the *Sunan* (sing. *Sunna*). There are different schools of law (*madhahib*, sing. *madhhab*) within Islam, which however are not *different legal systems*; they are *interpretations of the same laws*, each being a corpus of legal opinion with its own legal methodology and substantive principles,[22] which the Muslim follows (in Maltese we would use the phrase "*mexa ma*'", "*one goes along with*").[23] After the schools came into being, 'jurists began to be characterized as Hanafi, Maliki, Shafi'i or Hanbali, as determined by their *doctrinal* (not personal) loyalty to one school or another'[24] for the tasks of the jurist were 'to set forth a methodology by means of which a highly qualified jurist [could] discover God's law [... and to find] the justification and re-enactment of time-honored and long-established legal rules and of the processes of reasoning that produced and continued to sustain them. Put differently, this other role consisted of a reasoned defense of the *madhhab*, the legal school and its authoritative, standard doctrine'.[25]

Lay persons could follow any of these schools for a particular transaction or way of conduct, but each school ended up having influence in particular regions.[26] Indeed, the ideological map of the Islamic world is made up of the four *madhahib*: the Hanafi, Maliki, Shafi'i and Hanbali[27] and '[w]hile every region possessed its own distinct, practice-based legal system, there was nevertheless a multiplicity of study circles in each, and within each circle scholars disagreed on a wide variety of opinions.'[28] For instance, '[i]t has been

22 HALLAQ, WB (2009): *An Introduction to Islamic Law* Cambridge University Press, Cambridge, 34.

23 Note that this description applies to Sunni Islam, the dominant branch of Islam. Shi'a Islam takes a different approach.

24 *Loc. cit.*, 32.

25 HALLAQ, WB (1997): *History of Islamic Legal Theories* Cambridge University Press, Cambridge, ix.

26 HALLAQ, *op. cit.* (2009), 37.

27 *Loc. cit.*, 31. In the part of the Mediterranean which included Malta (comprising Malta, Sicily, Al-Andalus and the Far Maghreb), the Maliki *madhhab* was the dominant one (it still dominates in the Maghreb and Islamic Africa).

28 *Loc. cit.*, 36.

argued that a majority of Mālikīs of al-Andalus regarded opposing opinions within the school as possessing equal value. This "right to dissent" was not respected when a general consensus had been reached regarding the acceptance of one of the conflicting views. Therefore, Mālikīs did not recognize the right of zāhiris or pro-zāhiris to issue fatwas according to the doctrine of their *madhhab*, when this doctrine was viewed as contrary to the *sunna* and the *ijmā'*. The Mālikīs jealously protected the *sunna* at the same time that they defended the primacy of their school, and they were quick to take advantage of legal discrepancies to weaken their rivals.'[29]

2.2.2 *Madhhab* and the body politic

The creation of a *madhhab* was necessary for the legal class to achieve political prestige and authority, particularly since until modernity, the ruling classes in Islamic societies had very little, if anything, to do 'with the production and promulgation of legal knowledge or law'.[30] Yet law needed a source of authority, and the legal class proved to be that source which 'constituted an alternative to the authority of the body-politic; or, to put it more accurately, it came to fill a gap left untouched by Muslim rulers'.[31] Islamic law was not the product

> of the machinery of the body politic, but rather arose as a private enterprise initiated and developed by pious men who embarked on the study and elaboration of law as a religious activity. [...] The lack of governmental legal authority and power were made up for by the evolution and full emergence of the *madhhab*, an entity which came to possess even greater legal authority than that produced in other cultures by the body politic. If the body politic commanded obedience because it possessed political and coercive powers, the *madhhab* commanded a more evincive form of obedience because it spoke on behalf of God through his absolute

29 SERRANO, D (2000): "Legal Practice in an Andalusī-Maghribī Source from the Twelfth Century CE: The Madhāhib Al-ḥukkām fī Nawāzil al-Aḥkām", *Islamic L. & Soc'y* 187 Brill, The Netherlands, 232.

30 HALLAQ, *op. cit.* (2009), 36.

31 *Loc. cit.*, 37.

> *mujtahids*, those who *knew best* what God might have in mind as to what Muslims should or should not do. [...] This is not to say that the ruling elite did not have an important role to play (nevertheless, we must continue to insist that its role in *determining the role* was virtually nonexistent). [...] The legists constituted the linkage between [the political] elite and the masses, providing an efficient instrument to the ruling elite for gaining political control and legitimacy. Thus, inasmuch as the legists depended on the financial favors of those holding political power, the latter depended on the legists for accomplishing their own interests. [...] It was this reality – which made the approval of the men of law indispensable to the acts of politics – that gave formative Islam what we call today the rule of law. This model survived till the early twentieth century.[32]

2.2 The Hebrew *halakhah*

Halakhah has almost the same meaning like *madhhab*. It too derives from the verb "to go", *halakh*:[33]

> In the Bible the good life is frequently spoken of as a way in which men are "to go," e.g., 'and shalt show them the way wherein they are to go and the work that they must do' (Ex. 18:20). [... T]here developed the use of *halakhah* as a generic term for the whole legal system of Judaism.[34]

During the Middle Ages, legal theoreticians known as "decision-makers" (*posekim*) were asked to answer questions of interpretation of the Talmud and their *responsa* were collected, 'helping to form the basis for new codifications of the *halakhah*.'[35]

'*Halakhah* is the distinctive feature of Judaism as a religion of obedience to the word of God. It united Jews of many different temperaments, origins, and theological opinions.'[36] Yet, '[w]hereas "custom" (*minhag*) within the context of *national* legal systems

32 HALLAQ, *op. cit.* (2005), 205.

33 *Encyclopaedia Judaica* (Keter Publishing, Jersualem 1971) Vol. 7, 1156.

34 *Ibid.*

35 *Loc. cit.*, 1165.

36 *Loc. cit.*, 1166.

often refers to "local custom", for the *halakhah*, *minhag* often assumes a national dimension: *minhag ashkenaz*, etc.'.[37]

2.2.1 The three approaches to the *halakhah*

There are three approaches to the *halakhah*:

> The Orthodox rabbi, when faced with new halakhic problems ... will try to arrive at a decision by applying directly the ancient halakhic principles in the new circumstances. The Reform rabbi will be more inclined to consider the religious demands of the new age and will tend to operate within non-halakhic categories. The Conservative rabbi will try to utilize these latter in working out a fresh interpretation of the traditional *halakhah*.[38]

2.2.2 Legal pluralism and dissent

It is the modern, Western concept of law which prevails nowadays in Jewish law scholarship. However, within the *halakhah* 'a very different conception may be identified [...], one which adopts a pluralistic attitude towards the sources of Jewish law, and rejects the view that any valid application of the law must be justified by reliance upon those sources which are regarded, by the rules of the system, as the authoritative ones'.[39] The pluralistic legal structure means that 'the judge [in particular cases] choose[s] between two contradictory, but equally authoritative rules ... the "either-or" approach'.[40]

Three are the reasons why 'the rabbinic tradition of biblical law (*Halakhah*) [...] tolerates or even treasures dissent, though it possesses a transcendent law whose cultivation and recall is entirely the responsibility of scholars':

---

37 HECHT, N S ET AL.(ED.) (1996): *An Introduction to the History and Sources of Jewish Law* Oxford University Press, Oxford, 430.

38 *Ibid.*

39 Namely '(1) laws belong to a unified system; (2) within any such system, there are authoritative sources of law, and any valid application of the law must be justified by reliance upon those sources; (3) the system itself provides the means by which those rules may be recognised as authoritative' – HECHT ET AL., 421.

40 *Loc. cit.*, 427.

(i) 'because *Halakhah* itself is intrinsically open to disputation, the greatest text of rabbinic interpretation is fundamentally a record of contention';

(ii) 'though *Halakhah* has a transcendent origin, the rabbis recognized that the process of its working out is entirely a human affair, permitting no transcendent affirmation'; and

(iii) 'the recognition in *halakhic* tradition that, in theory at least, the view of a learned and pious dissenter may eventually win out over that of the majority'.[41]

3. Is "midheb" *madhhab* (or *halakhah*)?

Does *midheb* refer to the above? Do *lex propria* and *lex privata* (the definition given us by Vassalli) mean what the Muslims understand by *madhhab* and the Jews by *halakhah*?

Malta consistently presents a case of ambivalence: is she an Arab, Oriental country? Is she Christian/European? Or is she a hybrid, the Latinised Arab periphery, or the Arabised Latin periphery?[42]

The present author shall avoid entering into a discussion about the cross-fertilisation between "European" and Islamic laws from the eighth/ninth up to the eleventh/twelfth centuries (CE). Suffice it to mention, however, that scholars in this field argue not only that the English trial by jury derives from Islamic law,[43] but also other European institutes such as the *avallo* and *commenda*.[44]

---

41 JACOBSON, AJ (2005): "Publishing Dissent", 62 Wash. & Lee L. Rev. (Washington and Lee University, Lexington, Virgina 2005) 1610-13, 1615.

42 See RICH, PB (1998): "Racial ideas and the impact of imperialism in Europe" in *The European Legacy: Toward New Paradigms*, Vol. 3, No. 1, pp. 31-44 (Routledge, London 1998) 33 for an explanation 'on the periphery of the central imperial core of Latin Christendom' where 'a series of conquest states were created on the continental periphery which acted as a series of buffers'.

43 MAKDISI, JA (1998-1999): "The Islamic Origins of the Common Law", 77 N.C. L. Rev. (The University of North Carolina at Chapel Hill, Chapel Hill, North Carolina 1998-1999) 1635.

44 POTZ, R (2012): "Islam and Islamic Law in European Legal History" in *European History Online* (EGO) (Institute of European History (IEG), Mainz 2011-11-21). URL: http://www.ieg-ego.eu/potzr-2011a-en URN: urn:nbn:de:0159-2011112112 [2012-07-12] 6.

On the other hand, the Islamic *rahn* underwent a transformation, eventually ending up virtually mirroring the Roman *pignus*, which was a concept alien to Arabic law.[45] Furthermore, in Spain and Sicily, '[a]fter the Christian re-conquest, Arab-Islamic administrative structures were adopted, especially in the field of finance. After the Norman conquest of Sicily, not only were the administrative structures adopted but they developed into a whole, new, specific, remarkable, mixed Arab-Norman law [...]. As for al-Andalus, it is still not possible to definitively answer the question of the degree of influence exerted by Islamic law in Spain despite a number of recent studies on the subject'.[46]

The nest step is to propose an analysis of *lex propria*, *lex privata*, *usus* and *ritus*, expending some words on *consuetudo* too, and finally to compare them with *madhhab* (and *halakhah*).

4. Vassalli's definition: *Lex propria & privata*

Vassalli defines *midheb* as *lex propria & privata*. We stumble upon an obstacle when we try to define these terms because they were used for such a long time that their real meaning became blurred, a sort of "semantic entropy", as confirmed by the highly influential canonist Anacletus Reiffenstuel (1641-1703) in his classic work on Canon Law (the "other" of the two laws[47], the first one being the Civil Law):

> *Privilegium varia habet nomina in Jure, quae quasi sinonyma sunt. Quandoque enim vocatur jus singulare [...] indulgentia [...], exceptio [...], concessio [...], constitutio personalis [...], lex propria, l. municipalem [...], rescriptum [...], indultum [...]*[48]

45 SCHACHT, *op. cit.*, 16.

46 POTZ, *op. cit.*, 6.

47 *Utrumque jus.*

48 REIFFENSTUEL, A (1700/1834): *Jus canonicum universum* Dominicum Ercole, Rome, 334. [Privilege has various names in the Law, which are almost synonyms. Sometimes it is called *jus singulare* {...} *indulgentia* {...}, *exceptio* {...}, *concessio* {...}, *constitutio personalis* {...}, *lex propria, l. municipalem* {...}, *rescriptum* {...}, *indultum* {...}]

This confusion, this *entropy* as it were, is the hall-mark of the so-called "Middle Ages".[49] The present author would be tempted to apply to Vassalli Kenneth Pennington's persuasive argument about Thomas Aquinas, namely that the great medieval theologian mixed up *lex* and *ius* because he did not quite understand the legist Gratian.[50] But we shall resist this

49 It has been opined that it was an 'Enlightenment hope (or utopia)' that is was feasible to arrive 'at the possible remedy for disorder and confusion in laws, decisions, or doctrines' – BELLOMO, M (TRS. COCHRANE, L) (1995): *The Common Legal Past of Europe 1000-1800* The Catholic University of America Press, Washington D.C., 32. In other words, we seem condemned to thrive or perish in a juridical labyrinth of Greek Mythology proportions.

50 PENNINGTON, K (2008): "*Lex Naturalis* and *Ius Naturalis*" in *The Jurist* 68 University of Pittsburgh, Pittsburgh, 569 *et seq.*: 'The first jurist to examine *lex* and *ius* in detail was named Gratian who taught canon law in Bologna. In the first half of the twelfth century he compiled a *Tractatus de legibus* with which he introduced his students to law. He explored the different meanings of *ius* and *lex* for the first time in European jurisprudence. Gratian began his *Tractatus* with a statement that would remain a standard statement for centuries:
The Human Race is ruled by two things: namely, *natural ius* and *mos*. The *ius* of nature is what is contained in the *lex* and the Gospel. By it, each person is commanded to do to others what he wants done to himself and is prohibited from inflicting on others what he does not want done to himself. This indeed is the *lex* and the prophets.
[...] Gratian patterned his thought after texts that he found in Justinian's Digest. There he found a statement by the ancient jurist Gaius who also defined the law that governed human society:
All peoples who are ruled by *lex* and *mos* partly use their own *ius* and partly the *ius* that is common to all men. The *ius* that each nation has constituted for itself for each city is called the *ius civile*; almost as if it were a *ius proprium* of that city. What, however, the natural reason of men establishes and is used by all men equally, is called the *ius gentium*, almost as if all human beings use that *ius*.
Gaius began with *lex* but quickly switched his terminology to *ius*. *Ius* can be common to all men, but *ius* also governs each city. This *ius proprium* is also called *ius civile*.
[...] Gratian exploited another source, Isidore of Seville's *Etymologies* for much of his thinking about the two terms. Isidore discussed law in book five of his great encyclopedia, but his ideas about law did not enter into the Western tradition until Gratian.
He incorporated a text of Isidore in which a contrast was drawn between, *ius*, *mos*, and *lex*:
Consuetudo is a sort of *ius* established by *mos* and recognized as *lex* when *lex* is lacking. It does not matter whether it is confirmed by writing or by reason, since reason also supports *lex*. Furthermore, if *lex* is determined by reason, then *lex* will be all that reason has already confirmed – all, at least, that is congruent with reli-

temptation for the simple reason that Vassalli himself shows beyond the shadow of a doubt that he is aware of the difference: otherwise, why would he define *ħaqq* as *ius*, *quod iure debetur*, *gius*, *diritto*[51], *cosa dovuta*?

Also to be put aside are any and all religious connotations in Vassalli's definition. It is clear that by *lex privata*, Vassalli is not meaning here the medieval theological idea that *an individual* was exempt from the *lex publica* because of an order from God to behave in a particular way for a greater cause and the common good.[52] Otherwise, he would have said so explicitly instead of referring to the law and usages of *a people*.

4.1 What is *lex*?

Indeed, there are various contexts in which *lex* may be used: apart from juridical laws, there are laws of nature (as in the Galilean-Newtonian model of the Universe[53]), moral laws, social

---

gion, consistent with discipline, and helpful for salvation. *Consuetudo* is so called because it is in common use.

Custom was related to *ius* when grounded in *mos* and could be recognized as *lex* when there is no *lex*. Reason was the fundamental core principle of custom and *lex*.

[...]

When Thomas Aquinas discussed natural law in his *Summa theologiae* (ca. 1265-1272), he vacillated in his terminology between *ius naturale* and *lex naturalis*. As far as I can see, he used the two terms interchangeably, and he never drew upon the rich jurisprudential discussions of the meanings of "*ius*." Other evidence points to Thomas' having turned to and his becoming familiar with the legal tradition only in his later works. He cited Gratian's *Decretum* seven times in his *Commentary on the Sentences* and 81 times in his *Summa theologiae*.

It is not that Thomas was unaware or uninterested in law in his early writings. He cited papal decretals 32 times in his *Commentary on the Sentences*. I suspect that Thomas' own *Tractatus de legibus* forced him to confront Gratian's *Tractatus* as he was writing about law in his *Summa theologiae*.'

51 Let us not forget the ancient notarial formula, "*diritti, gius, pertinenze*" - which some notaries have carried on as "*drittijiet, ġus, pertinenzi*" or "*ġustijiet*". Also, a very minor but telling detail: Vassalli uses *diritto*, unlike Micallef who uses *Dritto*.

52 See *Joan of Arc and Spirituality* (ASTELL, A W & WHEELER, B (EDS.) (2003): Palgrave Macmillan, New York), especially the chapter entitled "Joan of Arc and the *Lex Privata*: A Spirit of Freedom in the Law" by J.M. Pinzino 85-110.

53 E.g. Newton's *Leges Motus*.

science laws (such as sociology).[54] Our interest is evidently circumscribed to juridical laws.

Strange but true, it seems that it is an absolutely arduous task defining "lex". Richeri's *Dictionarium Juris*,[55] for instance, omits to define the term by itself. *Lex* seems to be 'a ubiquitous term capable of both specialist and general meanings in Roman law.'[56] In its general meaning, Vicat[57] tells us, it refers to the law '*voluntatis imperantis, circa facienda vel omittenda a subditis declaratio*' ['a declaration of the ruler's will about the things that must be done or should not be done by (his) subjects'].

Although the etymology of the word *lex* is shrouded in uncertainty, it would seem that in an abstract sense it might refer to a "state of being", and on a more contrete level to an agreement which binds one legal subject to the will of another. Indeed, as Ulpian famously tells us,[58] contracts *accipiunt legem ex conventione*,[59] meaning that "contracts receive their *lex* from agreement".[60]

Then there is the conventionally drawn distinction 'between the use of the term *lex* in Roman public law (*lex publica*) and in private law (*lex privata/lex dicta*)'.[61] If we are left with the impression that instead of the order expected of the law we find ourselves astray in a dark wood, at least we find

54 Montesquieu's *De l'esprit des lois* is a precursor of modern socio-legal discourse.

55 Richeri (1792), a contemporary of Vassalli's. The author was not been able to find this dictionary in Malta, and had to go to Turin to consult it. However, Sir Adriano Dingli (1893) quotes Richeri in his *On the Force and Effects of Custom (Consuetudo) According to the Civil (Roman) Law* E. Laferla, Malta, 14, demonstrating that the Maltese were aware of him and used his books.

56 DU PLESSIS, PJ (2006): "The Roman Concept of lex contractus", 3 *Roman Legal Trad.* Roman Law Society of America, at the University of Kansas School of Law, Lawrence, Kansas 2006, 81.

57 VICAT, PH (1759): *Vocabularium Juris Utrisque* Bousquetania, Naples.

58 In D.16.3.1.6.

59 *Ulpianus libro trigensimo ad edictum: 'Si convenit, ut in deposito et culpa praestetur, rata est conventio: contractus enim legem ex conventione accipiunt'.*

60 DU PLESSIS, *op. cit.*, 82-83.

61 *Ibid.*, 81.

solace in the criticism levelled by Ludovico Antonio Muratori (1672-1750):

> *Non è più vero che s'abbia a ricorrere solamente al codice e ai digesti, per mettere fine alle controversie forensi. Quello è divenuto un picciolo, picciolissimo paese. Un altro senza alcun paragone più vasto è quello della giurisprudenza maneggiata dalle feconde e sottili menti dei giureconsulti degli ultimi secoli, i quali hanno anch'essi formato un altro sterminato corpo di leggi secondoché è sembrato al loro intendimento. E chiamo leggi le loro opinioni, perché a tenore di queste opinioni si regola il foro e si danno le sentenze ...*[62]

For others, things seem clearer. For instance, in Professor Pennington's words, medieval jurists (who were the point of departure of the *Ancien Régime* system) 'created a penumbra for *lex* that was concentrated not only on what was reasonable but also on consent.

Gratian was the first jurist in the European tradition who connected *lex* and consent. In a famous passage he declared that *leges* are established when they are promulgated, but that they are valid when they are approved by the *mos*[63] of those who use the *leges*'.[64] 'In contrast,' he continues, 'from early on, the penumbras of *ius* were justice, equity, and the common good'.[65]

4.2 *Ius*, or, The *Ancien Régime* system

Pennington draws our attention to the fact that medieval 'jurists never attributed the rich penumbras of meanings to *lex* that they did to *ius*. *Lex* was a plebian hod carrier of the law; *ius* was a term

---

62 Quoted by CAVANNA, A (1982): *Storia del diritto moderno in Europa: Le fonti e il pensiero giuridico 1* Giuffrè editore, Milan, 197. [It is not true that one has just to have recourse to the Code and the Digests to resolve judicial controversies. That has become a minute, very minute country. Instead, a bigger one, without equal, is the country of case-law moulded by the fertile and subtle minds of the jurisconsults of the last centuries, who have also formed an endless body of laws according to their intentions. I call their opinions laws because it is according to these opinions that judicial decisions are meted out.]

63 *Mos* is the singular of *mores*, meaning "tradition", "social norms".

64 PENNINGTON, *op. cit.*, 571.

65 *Ibid.*

rich in resonances. *Ius* reminded the jurists constantly of the transcendental significance of a legal system. It existed not just to establish right and wrong and to punish the wicked. It was the source of justice, equity, and rights'.[66]

Pennington is here referring to the systemic tension, as it were, between *ius* and *lex*, which for our purposes is important only insofar as it highlights the co-existence of a plurality of legal sources. To our modern understanding, this pluralistic system seems bizarre. To us moderns, the only recognizable source of law is the State.[67] There are of course different constitutional models

66 *Ibid.*

67 Says Cavanna: '... *fu appunto col progressivo accentrarsi dello Stato moderno, col crearsi di correnti dottrinali volte a giustificare il governo autocratico e quale risultato della politica statualistica, monocentrica e assolutista, che il concetto di un diritto comune, di un regime pluralistico di fonti e di una sua "gestione" giurisprudenziale iniziò ad entrare in crisi. Ad esso cominciò a contrapporsi il concetto via via più chiaro di un diritto come legge dello Stato sovrano nonchè l'immagine dello Stato stesso come produttore esclusivo e autoritario della norma giuridica anzichè come conservatore di un eterogeno e molteplice diritto precostituitogli. Lo Stato tese cioè a porsi come unica fonte del diritto (statualizzazione del diritto) e in ogni caso tese a condizionare la rilevanza giuridica di qualunque normativa interna o esterna non proveniente dal sovrano al requisito della recezione o del rinvio formale*' – CAVANNA, *op. cit.*, 193-194. ['... the concept of *ius commune*, that is a pluralistic regime of sources and of its "management" by means of case-law, entered its crisis precisely because of the progressive centralisation of the modern State. This entailed the creation of doctrinal currents aimed at justifying autocratic government and gave rise to statist, monocentric and absolutist policy. The competitor of the *ius commune* was the ever clearer concept of law as the law of the sovereign State, or rather the image of the State itself as exclusive and authoritarian producer of the juridical norm more than as keeper of a pre-existent heterogeneous and multifarious law. In other words, the State tended to present itself as the only source of law, and the nature of law became statist. The State tended to impose the requisite of reception or formal confirmation as a condition for the acceptance of the juridical relevance of any internal or external rule which did not emanate from the sovereign']. On the other hand, '*[o]ggi opportunamente si sottolinea che, spesso se non sempre, in età moderna lo Stato è piuttosto un luogo di mediazione e che l'accentramento è solo tendenziale, avviene faticosamente e con molti aspetti di empirismo e comunque in forme assai diseguali...*' – BIROCCHI, I (2006): 'La Formazione dei Diritti Patrî nell'Europa Moderna tra Politica dei Sovrani e Pensiero Giuspolitico, Prassi ed Insegnamento' in BIROCCHI, I & MATTONE, A (ED.) *Il diritto patrio: tra diritto comune e codificazione (secoli XVI-XIX)* Viella, Rome, 36 ['nowadays it is rightly underlined that, often if not always, in modern times the State is rather a place of mediation and that centralisation is only a tendency which requires a lot of effort and has many aspects of empiricism. All in all, it takes unequal forms ...'].

and theories of political philosophy which seek to legitimize this centralization of, or attempts at centralizing, law-production by the State, but these do not require our attention here since what is of the essence to our discussion is that the modern mind links 'law' only to the State.[68] Yet, before the rise of the modern State, there were numerous concurrent sources of law.[69] One such source was the *ius commune.*

Richeri tries to enlighten us: '*Jus commune interdum juri proprio cujusque civitatis opponitur & vulgo jus romanum significat*' and '*Commune jus vulgo romanum dicitur*' which, as Professor Zimmerman explains, 'found its manifestation in a very large, and essentially uniform, body of literature across Europe'. But Medieval Europe was characterised by dualism: Emperor and Pope, Roman (civil) law and Canon law, secular courts and ecclesiastical courts, legists (Roman law scholars) and canonists (Canon law scholars):

> There were jurisdictional shifts and conflicts that reflected the power politics between spiritual and secular rulers. But there were also far-reaching intellectual connections. Canon law was the law of the Roman Church, and it was largely based on Roman law; in turn, it exercised a considerable influence on the secular law. [...] Apart from Roman law and Canon law, there was the feudal law that had, however, been incorporated through the Libri feudorum into the body of Roman law. There were the systematic designs and the doctrines of the late scholastics in Spain and, later, of the

68 '... contrary to what occurs under the leaden cape of statutory law (in late modernity, for example), where the law becomes the expression of a centralized and centralizing will (legal monism), we will observe that the Middle Ages are, throughout, an age of legal pluralism. The medieval period demonstrates the possibility of the coexistence of diverse legal orders emanating from diverse social groups, even whilst the sovereignty of one political authority over the territory those groups inhabit remains unquestioned' – GROSSI, P (TRS. HOOPER, L.) (2010): *A History of European Law* Wiley-Blackwell, Chichester, United Kingdom, 4.

69 It is being argued that there is a return to pluralism, in Italy for instance, with the ongoing evolution '*che l'ordinamento italiano ha subito per effetto dell'inserimento del principio pluralistico fra i principî fondamentali della Costituzione*' – PIZZORUSSO, A (1998): 'Pluralismo delle fonti interne' in *Storia d'Italia (Annali 14): Legge Diritto Giustizia* Einaudi Editore, Turin, 1136 ['the Italian legal system has been affected by the insertion of the principle of pluralism among the fundamental principles of the Constitution'].

> adherents of a rationalistic Natural law that were moulded by Roman law and, in turn, influenced the *ius commune*. There were consuetudines (customs), confined in their application to specific places and territories, which were recognized within the framework of the *ius commune* and subjected to scholarly analysis. There were the rules and customary laws – predominantly unwritten but also sometimes laid down in writing – that had emerged, from about the twelfth century onwards...[70]

The *Ancien Régime* system was a complex system in which the *ius commune* served as the common law of Western Europe and different local laws obtained in each territory.[71]

Zimmerman tells us that 'there was an enormous variety of territorial and local legal sources that, in theory, always enjoyed precedence before the courts. For the *ius commune* was applicable only *in subsidio*, that is, as a subsidiary source of law. Yet, practically, it often gained the upper hand'.[72]

According to De Bono, the applicable Roman law (*ius commune*) in Malta was not what we find in Justinian's *Corpus iuris* but what was modified by the Canon Law, explained by the authors and received by the Courts.[73]

---

70 ZIMMERMAN, R (2007): "Roman Law and European Culture", New Zealand Law Review 341 Legal Research Foundation, Auckland, New Zealand, 362-364.

71 If one were to look for an analogy one might look at the Latin language – used throughout Western Europe – and the different languages and dialects all over the same territory. Indeed, it would seem that the history of languages and the history of laws run parallel to each other.

72 ZIMMERMANN, *op. cit.* (2007), 364.

73 '*Anche Baldo aveva scritto: Omnes populi possunt facere sibi statuta, et ubi cessat statutum habet locum ius civile (Ad L. 7, Dig. de inst. et iure). Si avverta, però, che il diritto comune, al quale si rapporta il codice, è meno quello che risulta dai testi del Corpus iuris, che quello che fu modificato dal diritto canonico, esposto dagli scrittori e ricevuto dall'uso del foro.*' – DE BONO, P, *op. cit.*, 211. ['Baldus too had written: All peoples are able to make for themselves statutes; where statutes cease there shall be the local *ius civile* (*Ad L. 7, Dig. de inst. et iure*). But a warning would be in place. The *ius commune* to which the Code belongs is not found in the text of the *Corpus iuris*, but in the modifications made by Canon Law as explained by writers and accepted by Court practice.']

5. Back to Vassalli, back to *midheb*

It is with this collage as background that we now go back to where we started, namely the term *midheb* and the two questions which urgently beg an answer: (i) what does the term mean? and (ii) does it indicate the existence of a non-Italianate Maltese legal terminology at the end of the 18th century? Vassalli tells us that *midheb* is *lex propria & privata* hinc *Lex & usus nationis, ritus.*

5.1 *Lex propria & privata*

In Vassalli's times, there was the crisis of the *ius commune* system. Muratori had already dealt his formidable blows, pushing the Prince to maintain no longer the respectful position of *conniventia principi*, but to intervene and amend the law.[74] Absolutism had grown so much that Revolutionary France beheaded its "despot". These were but the political symptoms of the socio-economic rise of the bourgeoisie, which required a different legal system for the new formation it required.[75] Yet, Vassalli's term *midheb* refers to pre-1789.

It refers to two ideas taken together, the law applicable to a territory (*lex propria*) and the law applicable between two or more private individuals resulting from an agreement (*lex privata*). These *leges* exist against the backdrop of the *ius commune*, the tapestry common to all of Western Europe. In the introduction to his annotated version of the Municipal Code (the *lex municipalis*[76]) of Malta, Micallef portrays this complex relationship when he describes the origins of the law and the ancient precedents, as well as '*il nesso col dritto romano – canonico – e siculo – le riforme e la nuova giurisprudenza – le consuetudini e gli usi dei Tribunali*'.[77]

74 The limitation on the number of generations in the institute of *fideicommissa* is the prime example of this new, legislatively active attitude.

75 The reader is referred to the excellent bird's eye-view in Chapter 6 of R. Lesaffer's (2009) *European Legal History: A Cultural and Political Perspective* Cambridge University Press, Cambridge, 372-480.

76 The Prince seems to have taken over completely the role of the *Universitas*.

77 MICALLEF, A (1841): *Dritto Municipale di Malta compilato sotto De Rohan G.M. Or Nuovamente Corredato di Annotazioni* Cumbo, Malta, xii. ['the link with Roman – Canon – and Sicilian law – the reforms and the new case-law – the customs

What Vassalli means is perhaps clarified by Professor Italo Birocchi:

> *Il processo di emersione di ciascun diritto territoriale impressiona meno per la quantità delle norme in questione, che pure, in diverse situazioni, è imponente, e più per la coscienza dei contemporanei che attorno a quel diritto si incardinasse il rispettivo ordinamento. Da qui l'esigenza, periodicamente rinnovata, di raccolta delle varie tipologie di fonti, più o meno ufficiali e corredate spesso di commentari.*
> *Di tali compilazioni la storiografia sottolinea, con ragione, le funzioni di accertamento e di razionalizzazione del diritto, ma forse queste possono dirsi comprese in un profilo più ampio, che è quello di "rappresentare" il diritto, cioè di manifestarlo in forma ordinata nella comunità politica come espressione di istituzioni e forze operanti nella società civile.* ***E infatti si raccoglie, o si progetta di raccogliere, di tutto: consuetudini, riti, statuti, ordini, formule negoziali, normative principesche.*** [Emphasis added.]
>
> *[...]*
>
> *Sotto questo profilo* ius patrium *[...] designa un insieme di fonti normative, evidentemente operanti entro un sistema pluralistico. Le fonti lo accreditavano come* ius commune *territoriale o anche* ius municipale *dell'ordinamento: termini antichi, come si vede, impiegati ora in un significato nuovo.*[78]

---

and the usages of the courts']

78 BIROCCHI, I, *op. cit.*, 34-35, 37 [Looking at the process whereby each territorial law emerged, one is not so impressed by the quantity of the norms in question, many of which were often impotent. One is certainly struck by the awareness of the people of the time that that territorial law was the lynch-pin of their own legal system. This explains the periodically-renewed need to collect all types of sources, in more or less official ways, and often to publish accompanying commentaries. Historiography rightly underlines that these compilations were meant to ascertain and streamline the law. But they had an even wider function, namely to "represent" the law, that is to show it in an orderly fashion to the political community as an expression of the institutions and forces working within civil society. **In fact there were collections of, or plans to collect, everything from customs, rites, statutes, orders,** ***formulae*** **relating to** ***negotia*****, to the laws made by the princes.** {...} Thus viewed, *ius patrium* [...] is an ensemble of sources of law evidently functioning in a pluralistic system. Historical sources say it was territorial *ius commune* or even the legal system's *ius municipale*. It is clear that these were ancient terms which were now given a new meaning.]

Lex nationis is the 'law' of the Prince, at times also a synonym of *lex municipalis*. The law of the Prince together with customary law (*usus nationis*) make the *lex propria* (the territorial, human law, applicable to *the entire people* of that territory) and the *lex privata* (the law created by common consent between *private individuals*, within the parameters of the entire system). In other words, the former is where the individual has no choice but to obey the dictates of the law, the latter where the individual may choose between different options. This law is different from the natural law, the *ius naturale* (*jedd*).

5.1.1 *Usus nationis*

When we read, in Notary Zabara's acts (1486-88) about the '*usum Melite*',[79] or in Court decisions of Vassalli's times about '*la nostra consuetudine*',[80] are we to infer that customs proper to the Maltese islands were referred to as *midheb*?[81]

79 See FIORINI, S (ED.) (1996): *Documentary Sources of Maltese History Part I: Notarial Documents No 1: Notary Giacomo Zabara R 494/1(I): 1486-1488* University of Malta Press, Malta - '*ad faldellas Jnsaccatum more Melite*' (deed 22, 24 April 1486); '*usum Gaudisij* (deed 44, 1 August 1486); '*usum Melite*' (deed 62, 6 September 1486); '*usum Melite*' (deed 63, 6 September 1486); '*more solito et consueto Melite*' (deed 92, 22 January 1487); '*usum et consuetu[dine]m Melite*' (deed 118, 9 February 1487); '*ut morjs est Melite*' (deed 279, 5 September 1487); '*usum Malte*' (deed 333, 9 February 1488) – where *more, usum, consuetudinem, morjs* all refer to customs.

80 See CARCERERI DE PRATI, C (2011): *Litium series rescisae: Le Decisiones del Supremo Magistrato di Giustizia di Malta nel Repertorio di Antonio Micallef* Jovene Editore, Naples - '*Il dotario è dovuto alla moglie vergine anche nei matrimoni secondo la consuetudine dei maltesi*' (**Rosa Ciumi v. Teresa Carnisi**, 31 October 1786, Registrum sententiarum, Vol. III, 277. 277); '*Un figlio od una figlia, secondo la consuetudine maltese, quante volte accetta l'assegnamento o la dote pro omni et quocumque jure, s'intende egli od essa ...*' (**Benigna v. Eredi Baldacchino**, 13 March 1784, Registrum sententiarum, Vol. II, 165.DCCLXIV); '*È d'uso, che ordinariamente le donne apportino al marito non solo la dote ma ...*' (**Creditori di Francesco Sillato v. Sillato**, 9 May 1789, Registrum sententiarum, Vol. II, 29.XII); '*In Malta le pensioni non si pagano di anticipato trattandosi di beni urbani, oltre i sei mesi, in pregiudizio del terzo; ma nel Gozo è costante l'antichissima consuetudine di pagarsi i fitti da anno in anno posticipatamente*' (12 April 1791); '*Nelle questioni circa la società coniugale si deve ricorrere al diritto commune quando nulla si rinviene stabilito dalla nostra consuetudine*' (25 August 1782); '*Nella società coniugale secondo la consuetudine il padre passando alle seconde nozze non perde l'usufrutto della terza materna e della terza figliale*' (21 June 1785) – *consuetudine* means *custom*.

81 As the reader will have gathered, it is being assumed throughout this essay

The answer is an unqualified yes. Customs would be part of the *lex propria.*

During Vassalli's lifetime, the legal landscape of the Maltese islands was a mixture of *lex scripta,* Maltese *consuetudo,* Sicilian *ius commune,* and the Roman-Canon *ius commune.* The existence of legal pluralism meant the *lex propria* of Malta – which undoubtedly was of the Maltese Islands and of the Maltese people – referred to, at the same time, Maltese law, Sicilian law, Roman and Greek law,[82] and Roman-Canon law.[83]

Indeed this interpretation seems to be corroborated by the harsh attacks made on Giandonato Rogadeo by his Maltese adversaries, namely that laws should be compiled by native lawyers who knew the country's spirit and character.[84] Words which echo Montesquieu, these.

---

that there was no evolution in the *Ancien Régime*, that the 300-year span between Zabara and the 18th-century Court's decisions was not characterized by significant tectonic plate movements. In actual fact, this is not exactly too much off the mark – orthodoxy holds that the real earthquake took place in 1789. On the other hand, however, it is incorrect to assume a static system before the French Revolution. If one were hard-pressed to find a more suitable metaphor than seismology, one could talk of a cauldron full of water put on the stove to boil. While the water is in its liquid state, its temperature changes continuously such that it is not a static system even though it is in the same state. When boiling point is reached, the water enters its gaseous state – it is still H_2O but in a different state and once again in a dynamic system. Cfr. Lesaffer, *supra.*

82 One finds in the *Codice Municipale di Malta* references to the usages of the Greeks and the Romans.

83 There are instances when reference was explicitly made to Sicilian law. For example, with regard to dower, Antonio Micallef says that '*ci regoliamo con gli usi siculi*' ['we follow Sicilian usages'] (MICALLEF, A, *op. cit.*, 398), probably referring to the *pretium virginis,* about which *vide* SICILIANO-VILLANUEVA, L (1901/1986): *Sul Diritto Greco-Romano Privato in Sicilia* Arnaldo Forni Editore, Sala Bolognese, 89. Yet, even here one has to tread with caution: which Sicilian customary law is reference really being made to? Certainly not the *iura propria* of the different Sicilian cities. Most probably, to the *ius commune* of Sicily, that mélange of Roman and Longobard laws which Frederick II claimed as "common" in his *Puritatem constitution* – CARCERERI DE PRATI, *op. cit.*, 30. Was that the Sicilian *midheb* (*vis-à-vis* the European *ius commune*)? All in all, Maltese law of that time can be seen as belonging to the 'legal kaleidoscope' (CALASSO, F (1954): *Medioevo del diritto,* I Le Fonti, Milan, 238) which was the Southern Italian world of law.

84 *Vide* CIAPPARA, F (2006): *Enlightenment and Reform in Malta 1740-1798* Midsea Books, Malta 66.

But we should also remember something else Montesquieu remarked, namely that Europe was one large State with many provinces. This acute remark conveys in a nutshell the *Ancien Régime* system: the *ius commune* applied (at least in theory) throughout Europe, while each different territory had its own laws, with a special relationship between the two laws.

With regard to the practice of the Courts, Zimmermann argues that the legal system prevailing until far into the eighteenth century allowed that 'where the law gives rise to ambiguity "*consuetudinem aut rerum perpetuo similiter iudicatarum auctoritatem vim leges optinere debere*" (statutory force ought to be ascribed to custom or to the authority of an unbroken line of similar judicial decisions)'.[85] Consequently, 'courts [...] displayed a flexible attitude towards precedents'[86]

> characterized by an interplay of individual legal maxims (*regulae iuris*), that aimed at "grasping the force and tendency of a statute rather than sticking to its words" and that was based, ultimately, on *aequitas* and *public utilitas*. [...] The period from the Middle Ages until the first third of the nineteenth century may be described as the age of equitable interpretation. The courts availed themselves of a wide range of legal maxims, they were guided by "the internal sense" of the law, and they were guided by the "equity of the statute" that could prevail even against its word.[87]

In this sense one could speak of an "opinion" – but it is the opinion of jurists, legists and judges.

5.1.2 *Ritus*

Richeri tells us that *ritus* '*aliquando significat solemnitates, aliquando mores, observationes*.' Vassalli is obviously referring to the second meaning. Also because he cross-references to *din* which he defines as *mos, ritus, consuetudo*. Once again the synonymy referred to

---

85 ZIMMERMANN, R (2001): *Roman Law, Contemporary Law, European Law: The Civilian Tradition Today* Oxford University Press, Oxford 178.

86 ZIMMERMANN, *loc. cit.*, 179.

87 ZIMMERMANN, *loc. cit.*, 182-183.

by Reiffenstuel becomes all too apparent. *Ritus* is (sometimes, *aliquando*) both *midheb* and *din*.

It is *mos* – social norms, tradition, the way things are done or the ritual – which makes custom legitimate. *Consuetudo*, tells us Richeri, '*est jus non scriptum moribus utentium comprobatum*' ['Customary law is the nwritten law that is sanctioned by the mores of those whom it serves']. He also gives us a definition of *jus scriptum*: '*quod est promulgatum, licet non sit scriptum, & ab hoc differt jus non scriptum seu consuetudo*' ['that law which has been promulgated, although it may not (necessarily) be written, & unwritten or customary law differs from this (type of law)'], which turns out to be a circular definition: custom is unwritten law confirmed by tradition, and written law is the law which is the contrary of unwritten law (or custom). When the written law came to a dead end, custom supplanted the necessary rules – even though there were tensions between the two, particularly when custom proposed a rule contrary to the written law, in which case the Prince would try to eradicate the custom. Yet, semantically speaking, the two terms, *lex* and *consuetudo* do not have the preciseness and rigidity which we today consider necessary. The terms were indeed used interchangeably – resulting in such "cocktails" as *lex consuetudinis* and *consuetudo et lex*, which defy contemporary expectations.[88]

The three most important attributes of *consuetudo* are (i) *antiquitas*,[89] (ii) the reference to the *natio* one belongs to,[90] and (iii) sacrality, indicated by the tie with *mores*.[91]

---

88 BALOSSINO, S (2005): "Iustitita, lex, consuetudo: per un vocabolario della giustizia nei capitolari italici", *Reti Medievali Rivista*, VI - 2005/1 (January-June) <http://www.dssg.unifi .it/_RM/rivista/saggi/Balossino.htm> (Firenze University Press, Florence 2005) accessed 12/08/2012.

89 In reality one might recall the 10-year period quoted by Sir Adriano Dingli in his late 19th-century book about matrimonial law in Malta – DINGLI, *op. cit.* ('IV. As to the length of time necessary to establish a cusom') 15–18.

90 In addition to the collocation *usum et consuetudinem terrae*, which attaches a custom to a land or territory thus becoming its characterising trait, there is the common usage of *consuetudo* to refer to groups who view themselves according to different ethnic tags (*consuetudo Francorum, consuetudo Langobardorum*) – BALOSSINO, *op. cit.*

91 BALOSSINO, *op. cit.*

5.2 Was there an 18th-century non-Italianate Maltese legal terminology?

From Vassalli's *Lexicon* it transpires that the answer is a definitive yes. Whereas he does not define the general meaning of *lex* (possibly to avoid entering the term *liġi*, which he would have considered a *vox non orientalis*), Vassalli does include the special meaning of each different *lex*. In addition to the entry *midheb*, he gives us *baqgħa, jedd, laqgħa* and *ħaqq*.[92]

5.2.1 *Baqgħa*[93]

'*II. Pactum, pactio, conventio, compositio; Patto, convenzione, accordo. Ġie waqt aqwa l-baqgħa mil-laqgħa: Aliquando fortiori est pactio, quam lex. Alle volte è più forte il patto della legge*' [Covenant, convention, agreement. Sometimes, agreement is stronger than law].[94] For Vassalli, there is an obvious difference between *midheb* (as *lex privata*) and *baqgħa* (as *pactum*). The difference is easily understood in the light of what has been said above: consent gives contracts (*pacti*) their *lex* (in the special meaning of *lex privata*). This term has survived in the notarial lexical register till this very day, when notaries use the formula, '***jibqa'*** *miftiehem bejn il-partijiet*', the equivalent of either *resta inteso tra le parti* or *le parti pattuiscono* [the parties agree].

5.2.2 *Jedd*

'*I. Ius naturale, nec non liberum arbitrium cuiusque; Diritto proprio e naturale, libero arbitrio II. Ius arbitrium in re* per vim; unde

92 Of these five terms, it seems only *midheb* has fallen in disuse, and for this reason this essay is limited only to its analysis, even though the other terms too provide scope for research and analysis.

93 It should be pointed out that *baqgħa* is, very likely, a local formation – in fact the three radicals of the Arabic root are B-Q-Y, which have been re-interpreted in Maltese as B-Q-Għ. Similarly, in the case of *laqgħa*, the three radicals of the Arabic root are L-Q-Y, which, in turn, have been re-interpreted in Maltese as L-Q-Għ.

94 Even here Aquilina (1987) fails to understand, translating this proverb as 'at times an agreement is more binding than the meeting (for the contract)' (*Maltese-English Dictionary*, Vol. I, Midsea, Valletta, 75) whereas Vassalli is clearly referring to *legge, lex* in the definition. Why should *legge* and *lex* be translated into 'the meeting (for the contract)' when it is clear from the definition of *laqgħa* that its meaning is deeper?

ius subiectionis, dominationis, summum ius in rebus, summum imperium in hominibus' ['I. Natural law and also the free will of each (man). II. The *ius arbitrium* through the use of force; whence *ius subiectionis, dominationis*, the highest right on things, the highest power on men'].

The second meaning is the power (the right) one has on something or somebody else. To put it succinctly, the first meaning, *ius naturale*, denotes the law emanating from nature filtered through human reason.

By Vassalli's time, natural law had been subjected not only to the rigorous abstractions born of the idea that law could emulate science and find universal rules which applied to all humanity, but also to a nascent legal absolutism, whence the Prince would write the laws, because the only thing he would have in mind would be the public good.

The irony of this view lay in the Prince being the sovereign of a small stretch of territory; the ideals of universalism would thus be implemented by a fragmented system of political units. This then required the imposition of a uniform law over bigger political units, namely the centralised States.

But most importantly, Enlightenment thinkers – who mostly belonged to Masonic lodges or other exclusive groupings – disdained the common people and therefore the law which emanated from their behaviour (*consuetudo*) and the jurists who interpreted it. Much of this was due to the fact that by Vassalli's time, property had been declared "sacred" – not religiously but legally – and therefore all that would be done to safeguard it would be in the public good.[95] We can only surmise what Vassalli's views were about all this; but what we can say for sure is that the term *ius naturale* too underwent a semantic shift over time.

5.2.3 *Laqgħa*

'II. *Unio, conventio: it. Adunanza di persone, convenzione.* Hinc *Lex* spec. *Municipalis; legge municipale, e specialmente (secondo la forza di questa dizione) fatta e promulgata in un'adunanza*' ['An assembly, a convention of persons; whence *law*, specifically

95 See GROSSI, *op. cit.* 2010, 59-69.

Municipalis; municipal law, in particular made and promulgated during an assembly'].

Richeri defines *lex municipalis* as '*lex municipalis stricte sumta est, quae cuique municipio propria est. – late significat ditionis alicujus leges. Municipale, quod ad municipium pertinet: ita municipalis lex, quae est propria cujusque municipii. Municipes hodie dicimus cujusque universitatis cives*' ['Municipal law, in its narrowest sense, is assumed to be that which belongs to each *municipium* – in a wide sense, it means laws of any body that has sovereign power. *Municipale*, that which applies to a *municipium*. Thus is the municipal law, which belongs to each *municipium*. Today, we call "*municipes*" those who are citizens of a corporate body'].

5.2.4 *Ħaqq*

'*I. verum, il vero. II. Veritas & iustitia, verità, giustizia. III. Ius, quod iure debetur, gius, diritto, cosa dovuta. [...] VI. tribunal, forum, curia, foro, tribunale, curia*' [I. Truth. II. Truth and justice. III. Law, what is owed by law. {...} VI. Court of law, tribunal].

5.2.5 Taken all together

Indeed, if *laqgħa* is *lex municipalis* and *din* is *consuetudo*, then *laqgħa* + *din* = *midheb* (*lex propria*).

Baqgħa (*pactum*) within the limits allowed by the *midheb* and the *jedd* (in the complex relationship that existed between them) would give rise to the *lex privata*, also *midheb*.

Would *midheb* be in conterposition to *jedd*?

Would all be included in *ħaqq*?

Would lawyers and the establishment have used such language?

Vassalli did not want to '*dilungare l'argomento*'.[96]

Perhaps now is the moment to heed the advice of the old man, and leave these questions for others to answer.

96 See fn. 3 above.

5.3 Could it be that *midheb* was coined by Vassalli himself?

It cannot be categorically excluded. But the present author would tend toward a negative answer, for the following reasons:

(i) In the case of *Malek* (= *Rex*) Vassalli clearly states that it is a '*parola in oggi disusata*' ['this word is no longer used'] but then justifies its inclusion on the basis that it appears in a Phoenician inscription found in 1761 at Ta' Bengħajsa. Vassalli here enthusiastically includes a term which supports his thesis on the origins of the Maltese language; why should he then coin a term patently unuseful to his basic thesis?

(ii) Could it be that Vassalli was trying to find a pure word (which would not be a *vox non orientalis*) instead of using *liġi* [law]? I doubt it. First, because he has no qualms with *pleġġ* (*malleveria, garanzia, sigurtà*) [surety], *renta* (*proventus, sensus, provento, rendita, entrata*) [annuity], and *talja* (*pena pecuniaria*) [pecuniary sanction]. And secondly, because he does not propose Semitic nouns for *avvocato*,[97] *procuratore del fisco, uditore* [advocate, public prosecutor, publicly-employed lawyer entrusted with certain judicial functions]. Whereas he could have easily coined terms derived from the Arabic محام (*muham*), he just omitted those three words. Why should he have behaved differently with *midheb*?

(iii) In the case of *apostolus* [apostle], Vassalli does prefer *rasul* but he lists *apostlu* (sic) too. Why act differently with *midheb*?

6. Parting shot: a very brief comparison between the European-Christian legal mentality and the Islamic legal mentality

As we have seen above, the ruling classes in Islamic societies had very little, if anything, to do 'with the production and promulgation of legal knowledge or law'. This was also the case with the *Ancien Régime*, in which the role of the political class in the production

97 Not even *evokat* or *evukat* (on the model of *Evyssu – Awwissu*).

of law underwent a process of growth over time, a sort of cancer which ultimately brought about the body's death.[98]

We have also seen that in Islamic societies law was produced by pious men learned in the law; similarly, throughout the European Middle Ages, the civil (or Roman) law was constantly influenced by Canon Law and it was a learned law, sustained by academic scholarship and study'.[99] Indeed, as the 12th-century Roman jurist Azo explains: 'A *lex* is the common opinion of men who are learned in the law...'[100]

There are indeed similarities – at least *prima facie* – between these two worlds.

7. Conclusion: Latin wine, Semitic decanter

Owing to their Christian traditions, the Maltese have a word for *lent*. Like so many other cases, it is a local variant of an Arabic word, in this case *randan* from *ramadan*. It is however common knowledge that the Maltese do not behave during the *randan* as the Muslims behave during the *ramadan*. Similarly, *midheb* is the Maltese variant of the Arabic *madhhab*, but despite the possible similarities between the two concepts, the Maltese notion is Christian-European whereas the Arabic notion is Islamic. Indeed, Latin wine decanted in a Semitic carafe. Or, a fusion of cultures.

98 This is the metaphor GROSSI, *op. cit.* (1995), uses.

99 ZIMMERMANN, *op. cit.* (2006), 362.

100 PENNINGTON, *op. cit.* Azo also said, '*Lex* is sometimes defined narrowly and sometimes broadly. An example of a narrow definition is when a statute of the Roman people is called a *lex*. [...] *Lex* is broadly defined when it is used to describe all reasonable statutes. Whence *lex* is a sacred command, ordering honesty and prohibiting the contrary'.

Bibliography

Judicial Importation into Maltese Law of Italian Private Law Solutions and Its Implications

Books

BILLIET, C (1896): *Lois Civiles de Malte Traduites et annotées et mises en concordance avec le code français, Traduction publiée avec l'autorisation de M. le Premier Président de la Cour d'appel d'Alger*, Collect. de Codes Étrangers XVII Paris Pedone, Paris

FERRANTE, R (2002): *Dans l'ordre établi par le Code civil. La scienza del diritto al tramonto dell'Illuminismo giuridico* Giuffrè, Milan

--------------- (2011): *Codificazione e cultura giuridica* 2nd ed, Giappichelli, Turin

GROSSI, P (2007): *Società, Diritto, Stato. Un recupero per il diritto* Giuffrè, Milan

LARENZ, K (2008): *Methodenlehre der Rechtswissenschaft* 1st ed., Springer Berlin Heidelberg, Berlin

LESAFFER, R (2009): *European Legal History A Cultural and Political Perspective* Cambridge University Press, Cambridge

MARKESINIS, B & FEDTKE, J (2006): *Judicial Recourse to Foreign Law. A New Source of Inspiration?* Routledge, Oxford

MIFSUD BONNICI, U (2004): *An Introduction to Comparative Law* Malta University Press, Malta

Chapters in books

HAGE, J (2009): 'What is a legal transaction?' in DEL MAR, M & BANKOWSKI, Z (EDS.): *Law as Institutional Normative Order* Ashgate, Surrey

HALSON, R & CAMPBELL, D (2013): 'Harmonisation and its discontents: a transaction costs critique of a European contract law' in DEVENNEY, J & KENNY, M (EDS.), *The Transformation of European Private Law Harmonisation, Consolidation, Codification or Chaos?* Cambridge University Press, Cambridge

HARDING, H W (1994): 'Law' in FRENDO, H & FRIGGIERI, O (EDS.): *Malta Culture and Identity* Ministry for Culture and the Youth, Malta

POZZO, B (2006): 'Multilingualism, Legal Terminology and the Problems of Harmonising European Private Law' in POZZO B ET AL. (EDS.): *Multilingualism and the Harmonisation of European Law* Kluwer Law International, The Hague

Articles in journals

ANDÒ, B (2011): 'The Role of Judges in Mixed Legal Systems' [2011] *Journal of Civil Law Studies* Vol 4 Issue 2

BARKHUYSEN, T, VAN EMMERIK, VL, & UZMAN, J (2010): 'The Dutch Supreme Court: A Reluctant Positive Legislator?' [2010] *Electronic Journal of Comparative Law* Vol 14.3 <http://www.ejcl.org/143/art143-16.pdf> accessed 3 February 2015

Unpublished materials

GALEA, P: Unpublished lectures on Prolegomena, University of Malta

Court cases

Galea vs Falzon, Court of Appeal (Civil), 9 October 2009

Historical Facts and Myths surrounding the Criminal Code of Malta

Books

ANON. (1870): *Annotazioni alle Leggi Criminali per l'Isola di Malta e Sue Dipendenze da Servire di Guida al Giurato per cura d'un giovane Avvocato maltese*, Tipo-Litografia Anglo-Maltese, Valletta

ASHCROFT, B (2001): *On post-colonial futures: transformations of colonial culture* Continuum International Publishing Group, New York

BELLOMO, M (TRS. COCHRANE, L) (1995): *The Common Legal Past of Europe* The Catholic University of America Press, Washington D.C.

BIGELOW, A (1831): *Travels in Malta and Sicily: with sketches of Gibraltar in 1827* Carter, Hendee & Babcock, Boston

BERTOLOTTI, D (1838): *Gli Arabi in Italia* Baglione, Turin

BRYDONE, P (1773): *A Tour through Sicily and Malta in a Series of Letters to William Beckford, Esq. of Somerly in Suffolk.* Vol. I W. Strahan and T. Cadell, London

CAVANNA, A (1982): *Storia del Diritto Moderno in Europa. Le fonti e il pensiero giuridico* Giuffrè editore, Milan

CIAPPARA, F (2006): *Enlightenment and Reform in Malta 1740-1798* Midsea Books, Santa Venera, Malta

CREMONA, JJ (1990): *Selected Papers 1946-1989* Publishers Enterprises Group, Marsa, Malta

---------------- (1994): *The Maltese Constitution and Constitutional History Since 1813* Publishers Enterprises Group, San Ġwann, Malta

DAVIS, JA (2006): *Naples and Napoleon. Southern Italy and the European Revolutions*, 1780-1860 Oxford University Press, Oxford

DE BONO P (1897): *Sommario della Storia della Legislazione in Malta* Tipografia del Malta, Valletta

DE CARO, A (1845): *Il Processo Criminale in Malta* Valletta

GORDON, GH (1967): *The Criminal Law of Scotland* 1st ed., W. Green & Son Ltd/Scottish Universities Law Institute, Edinburgh

GOURLAY, D (2015): *Sheriff Andrew Jameson. The Life of Effie Gray's Uncle* Melrose Books, United Kingdom

GREGORY, D (1996): *Malta, Britain and the European Powers, 1793-1815* Associated University Presses, Inc., Cranbury, New Jersey

HOUGH, B & DAVIS, H (2010): *Coleridge's Law. A Study of Coleridge in Malta* Open Book Publishers, Cambridge

JACKSON, LA (2000): *Child Sexual Abuse in Victorian England* Routledge, Oxford

JAMESON, A (1844): *Report on the Proposed Code of Criminal Laws for the Island of Malta and its Dependencies* Government Press, Malta

JONES, TH & CHRISTIE, MGA (2003): *Greens Concise Scots Law Criminal Law* 3rd ed. Thomson, Edinburgh

KODITSCHEK, TH (2011): *Liberalism, Imperialism, and the Historical Imagination* Cambridge University Press, New York

KOSKENNIEMI, M (2004): *The Gentle Civilizer of Nations. The Rise and Fall of International Law 1870-1960* Cambridge University Press, Cambridge

MAHOOD, L (1990): *The Magdalenes. Prostitution in the Nineteenth Century* Routledge, London

MILL, JS (1868/1992): *England and Ireland* Collected Works Toronto University Press, Toronto

MITCHELL, JP (2002): *Ambivalent Europeans. Ritual, Memory and the Public Sphere in Malta* Routledge, London

MONTAIGNE, M (TRS. SCREECH, MA) (2003): *The Complete Essays* Penguin, London

PORTER, R (1991): *English Society in the Eighteenth Century* Penguin Books, London

QUATRIGLIO, G (1996/1999): *Mille Anni in Sicilia. Dagli Arabi ai Borboni* Marsilio, Venice

ROBINSON, OF, FERGUS, TD, GORDON, WM (2000): *European Legal History* Butterworths, London-Edinburgh-Dublin

ROSSELLI, J (1956): *Lord William Bentinck & the British Occupation of Sicily 1811-1814* Cambridge University Press, Cambridge

---------------- (1974): *Lord William Bentick: the making of a liberal imperialist* Sussex University Press, Edinburgh

SAID, E W (2003 ED.): *Orientalism* Penguin, London

SAPIR, E (1993 ED.): *The Psychology of Culture* Mouten de Guyter, Berlin

SERPENTINI, A L (ED.) (2006): *Dictionnaire Historique de la Corse* Albiana, Ajaccio, France

SMITH, T B (1962): *Short Commentary on the Law of Scotland* W. Green, Edinburgh

STEIN, P (1999): *Roman Law in European History* Cambridge University Press, Cambridge

STEWART, F H (1994): *Honor* University of Chicago Press, Chicago-London

SUPIOT, A (TRS. BROWN, S) (2007): *Homo Juridicus. On the Anthropological Function of the Law* Verso, London-New York

ULLMAN, W (1946): *The Medieval Idea of Law as Represented by Lucas de Penna* Methuen & Co. Ltd., London

ZIMMERMANN, R (2001): *Roman Law, Contemporary Law, European Law. The Civilian Tradition Today* Oxford University Press, Oxford

Chapters in books

COLAO, F (2008): 'Carrara e alcuni «Delitti di Pericolo Comune» del Codice

Jonio' in VINCIGUERRA: *Codice Penale degli Stati Uniti delle Isole Jonie (1841)* CEDAM, Padua

DEZZA, E (2003): '... Felicemente disposano le tradizioni della scuola italiana alle libertà inglesi' in VINCIGUERRA, S (ED.), *Leggi Criminali per l'Isola di Malta e Sue Dipendenze (1854)* CEDAM, Padua

------------ (2008): 'Istituti di Common Law nel Codice di Procedura Penale Jonio' in VINCIGUERRA: *Codice Penale degli Stati Uniti delle Isole Jonie (1841)* CEDAM, Padua

DI RENZO VILLATA, M G (2003): "Da Filangieri a Malta: Il Caso del Furto" in VINCIGUERRA (ED.), *Leggi Criminali per l'Isola di Malta e Sue Dipendenze (1854)* CEDAM, Padua

GANADO, A (2003): 'La Storia del Codice Penale di Malta del 1854. Un breve ragguaglio' in VINCIGUERRA: *Leggi Criminali per l'Isola di Malta e Sue Dipendenze (1854)* CEDAM, Padua

GANE, C (2005): 'Civilian and English influences on Scots Criminal Law' in REID, E, ET AL (EDS.): *A Mixed Legal System in Transition. TB Smith and the Progress of Scots Law* Edinburgh University Press, Edinburgh

LUPARIA, L & GARBAGNATI, G (2003): 'Il Processo Penale Maltese tra Modello Adversary e Radici Continentali' in VINCIGUERRA: *Leggi Criminali per l'Isola di Malta e Sue Dipendenze (1854)* CEDAM, Padua

MANGION, R. (2009), "Professors who Taught International Law within the Faculty of Laws, University of Malta" in MARTINEZ GUTIÉRREZ, N.A. (ED.), *Serving the Rule of International Law: Essays in Honour of Professor David Joseph Attard*, Mare Nostrum Publications, Malta

NOVARESE, D (1998): 'Tra Francia e Inghilterra. Riflessioni siciliane sulla carta del 1812' in ROMANO, A (ED.): *Il Modello Costituzionale Inglese e la sua Recezione nell'Area mediterranea tra la Fine del '700 e la prima Metà dell' '800* Giuffrè editore, Milan

NOVARESE, D (2003): 'Istanze costituzionali e codificazione a Malta nel secolo XIX. Le origini del codice penale del 1854' in VINCIGUERRA, S (ED.), *Leggi Criminali per l'Isola di Malta e Sue Dipendenze (1854)* CEDAM, Padua

PADOA-SCHIOPPA, A (2003): 'La Giuria Penale a Malta 1811-1854)' in VINCIGUERRA, S: *Leggi Criminali per l'Isola di Malta e Sue Dipendenze (1854)* CEDAM, Padua

STEWART, CH (2002): 'The Mediterranean as a culture area' in BARNARD, A & J. SPENCER, J (EDS.), *Encyclopedia of Social and Cultural anthropology* Routledge, London

VELLA, M (2009): 'The economics of hypocrisy – deconstructing half a century of development discourse in Malta – notes on work in progress' in CASSAR, G *ET AL* (EDS.): *Social Transitions in Maltese Society* Agenda, Ħal Luqa, Malta

VINCIGUERRA, S (2008): 'Umanità delle Pene Detentive, Prevenzione del Reato e Ristoro del Danno' in VINCIGUERRA, S (ED.): *Codice Penale degli Stati Uniti delle Isole Jonie (1841)* CEDAM, Padua

WILSON, WA (1992): 'The Importance of Analysis' in CAREY MILLER, D L & D.W. MEYERS, D W (EDS.): *Comparative and Historical Essays in Scots Law* Butterworths & The Law Society of Scotland, Edinburgh

Articles in journals

ANON. (1806): 'Remarks on Malta and Sicily' in *The Monthly Magazine*, Vol. XX. Richard Phillips, London

ANON. (1844): 'A Supplement to Hume's Commentaries on the Law of Scotland respecting Crimes' in *The North British Review*, Vol. IV, November 1845-February 1846 W.P. Kennedy, Edinburgh

BAUMAN, R A (1983): "Grotius: Father of Roman-Dutch Law?" in 1983 *Bull. Austl. Soc. Leg. Phil.*, no. 26 Australian Society of Legal Philosophy, Canberra

CAREY MILLER, D L (1992): 'Systems of Property: Grotius and Stair' in CAREY MILLER, D L & D.W. MEYERS, D W (EDS.): *Comparative and Historical Essays in Scots Law* Butterworths & The Law Society of Scotland, Edinburgh

GANADO, A (1949): 'The Historical Development of the Criminal Code' in *Law Journal*, Nos. 4, 5, and 6 University Student's Law Society, Valletta 1949-1950

GOURLAY, D (2010): "Andrew Jameson and the Origins of the Criminal Code of Malta" in *Melita Historica*, Vol. XV, no. 2

LEE, H I (1964): 'British Policy towards the Religion, ancient Laws and Customs in Malta 1824-1851' in *Melita Historica*, 4(1964)1, http//www.judiciarymalta.gov.mt/file.aspx?f=442 accessed 20 August 2011

NOVARESE, D (2002): 'Fra Common Law e Civil Law. Il Jury nell'Esperienza Costituzionale Siciliana 1810-1815)' in *Historia Constitucional. Revista electrónica*, No. 3, June 2002, Spain http//www.seminariomartinezmarina.com/ojs/index.php/historiaconstitucional/article/viewFile/177/157accessed 11 August 2011

Legislative materials

Debates, Italian Chamber of Deputies, 24 October 1969

Dritto Municipale di Malta Compilato Sotto De Rohan G.M. Or Nuovamente Corredato di Annotazioni Francesco Cumbo, Malta 1841, Tome I

The Tuscan Code (or *Leopoldino*), Siena 1786

Other materials

BORG, T (2010): 'Malta, France and UK: Legacy in History' in *The Times* Allied Newspapers, Valletta 4 December 2010

GOURLAY, D (2010): "Andrew Jameson (1811-1870)" paper presented at the Conference *Andrew Jameson: a Scottish eye to the Mediterranean Law Experience* organized by the University of Padua and the Robert Gordon University of Aberdeen, in Padua 12-13 March 2010

SAMMUT, F (2011): 'Reluctant to serve as jurors' in *The Times* Allied Newspapers, Valletta 9 October 2011

Medieval (Legal) Beasts in our Midst? A Terminological *Ad Fontes* Look at the Dissolution of Contracts under Maltese Law

Books

ANON (1803): *Guide des Notaires et des Employés de l'Enregistrement*, Vol. III 2nd ed., Bureau des Instructions Decadaires, Paris

ANON (1828): *Annali Universali di Agricoltura, Economia Rurale e Domestica Ed Arti e Mestieri*, Vol. 7 Editori degli Annali Universali delle Scienze e dell'Industria, Milan

BARGELLI, E (2010): *Il Sinallagma Rovesciato* Giuffrè, Milan

BETTINI, F (1857): *Giurisprudenza degli Stati Sardi. Raccolta Generale Progressiva di Giurisprudenza, Legislazione e Dottrina* Unione Tipografica-Editrice, Turin

BOYER, G (1924): *Recherches Historiques sur la Résolution des Contrats (Origines de l'Article 1184 C. Civ.)* Les Presses Universitaires de France, Paris

CARONI, P (1998): Saggi *sulla Storia della Codificazione* Giuffrè Editore, Milan

CUSHING, W (1889): *Anonyms: A Dictionary of Revealed Authorship* Cambridge, Massachusetts

HALKETT, S & LAING, J (1883): *Dictionary of Anonymous and Pseudonymous Literature of Great Britain* William Paterson, Edinburgh

CORNU, G (1987): *Vocabulaire juridique* PUF, Paris

DEZZA, E (2000): *Lezioni di Storia della codificazione civile* 2nd ed, Giappichelli Editore, Turin

DOMAT, J (1822): *Lois civiles, Des engagements* Livre I Paris

DU MOLIN, MC (1678): *Coustumes de la Prevosté et Vicomté de Paris*, André Soubron, Paris

DUPIN SENIORE (1842): *Opere di G.R. Pothier contenenti i trattati del Diritto francese*, Seconda Edizione Italiana, Tomo Secondo Vignozzi, Leghorn

DURANTON, A (1848): *Corso di diritto civile secondo il codice francese*, Vol. IX, Titolo VI - *Del contratto di vendita* 2nd ed., Domenico Capasso Libraio-Tipografo-Editore, Naples

FAVATA, A (2003): *Dizionario dei termini giuridici* La Tribuna, Pia-cenza

FERRANTE, R (2011): *Codificazione e cultura giuridica* Giappichelli Editore, Turin

GIORGI, G (1898): *Teoria delle obbligazioni nel diritto moderno italiano*, Vol. IV - *Delle obbligazioni condizionali, § VII - Della condizione risolutiva tacita* 5th ed., Casa Editrice Libraria Fratelli Camelli, Florence

GIORDANO, A (1858): *Comento* [sic] *sulle Leggi Civili del Regno delle Due Sicilie*, Vol. III Fibreno, Naples

GENTILI, A (1990): *La risoluzione parziale* Jovene, Naples

GUILLIEN, R & VINCENT, J (2003): *Lexique des termes juridiques* Dalloz, Paris

HALPÉRIN, JL (1996): *Histoire des Droits en Europe de 1750 à nos jours* Flammarion, Paris

LAURENT, F (1882): *Corso elementare di diritto civile,*Vol. XXV. *Estinzione del contratto d'affitto, § III Conseguenze della risoluzione* Naples

LESAFFER, R (2009): *European Legal History: A cultural and political perspective* Cambridge University Press, Cambridge

MALAURIE, P & AYNES, L (1998-99): *Cours de droit civil, Les obligations* Cujas, Paris

MANTELLI, C (1844): *Giurisprudenza del Codice Civile e delle Altre Leggi dei Regii Stati ossia Collezione Metodica e Progressiva delle Decisioni e Sentenze Pronunciate dai Supremi Magistrati sì dello Stato che stranieri ecc* Luigi Guidetti, Alessandria

MELANO DI PORTULA, A (1859): *Dizionario Analitico di Diritto e di Economia Industriale e Commerciale* Giuseppe Cerutti, Turin

MOSCO, L (1950): *La risoluzione del Contratto per Inadempimento* Jovene, Naples

MOURLON, F (1863): *Répétitions Écrites sur le Troisième Examen du Code Napoléon contenant l'Exposé of sale agreementé des Principes Généraux* A Maresq, Paris

NAZ, L (1870): *Essai sur l'Histoire de la Résolution de la Vente pour défaut de paiement du prix et son état dans le droit français moderne* Durand and Pédone-Lauriel, Paris

NUGENT, TH (1808): *The New Pocket Dictionary of the French and English Languages* 12th ed., Flint, London

PACIFICI-MAZZONI, E (1882): *Codice Civile Commentato con la Legge Romana, le Sentenze dei Dottori e la Giurisprudenza – Trattato della Vendita* Vol. I 2nd ed., Cammelli, Florence

PASINI, J (1814): *Vocabularium Latino-Italicum* Parolari, Venice

SALZANO, TMV (1834): *Lezioni di Diritto Canonico Pubblico, e Privato Considerato in Sè Stesso e Secondo l'Attual Polizia del Regno delle Due Sicilie,* Vol. III 2nd ed., Saverio Giordano, Naples

SCLOPIS, F (1864): *Storia della legislazione italiana, III, Dall'epoca della Rivoluzione Francese, 1789 a quella delle riforme italiane, 1847* Unione Tipografica-Editrice, Turin

SCHELER, A (1862): *Dictionnaire d'Étymologie Française* Didot, Paris

STARCK, B (1972): *Droit civil* Librairies techniques, Paris

TORTORA, G (1994): *Dizionario Giuridico Italiano-Francese Francese-Italiano* 3rd ed., Giuffrè, Milan

TILLEMAN, BT, VERBEKE, AL, VERKINDT, PY (2006): *Droit des contrats,* France Belgique Larcier, Brussels

TORRENTE, A & SCHLESINGER, P (2011): *Manuale di diritto privato* 20th ed., Giuffrè, Milan

ZACHARIÆ, CS (1845): *Corso di Diritto Civile Francese, Prima Traduzione Italiana, Colla Concordanza degli Articoli del Codice Civile per gli Stati di S.M. il Re di Sardegna* Libreria della Minerva Subalpina, Turin

Articles in books

DEZZA, E (2000): 'Giuseppe Luosi e il "Codice Napoleone Italiano". Cronaca di una breve illusione' in TAVILLA, E (ED.), *Giuseppe Luosi, giurista italiano ed europeo. Traduzioni, tradizioni e tradimenti della codificazione* Quaderni dell'Archivio Storico, Modena

FERRANTE, R (2009): 'Traduzione del codice e tradizione scientifica: la cultura giuridica italiana davanti al Codice Napoleone' in TAVILLA, E (ED.), *Giuseppe Luosi, giurista italiano ed europeo. Traduzioni, tradizioni e tradimenti della codificazione* Quaderni dell'Archivio Storico, Modena

HARDING, HW (1994): 'Law' in FRENDO, H & FRIGGIERI, O (EDS.), *Malta: Culture and Identity* Ministry of Youth and the Arts, Malta

HALPÉRIN, JL (2009): 'A proposito di alcune difficoltà nell'applicazione dei codici napoleonici nei dipartimenti francesi d'Italia' in TAVILLA, E (ED.), *Giuseppe Luosi, giurista italiano ed europeo. Traduzioni, tradizioni e tradimenti della codificazione* Quaderni dell'Archivio Storico, Modena

Articles in journals

CURY, J (2009): 'Resolución, Rescisión, Resiliación y Nulidad' Dominican Republic <www.jottincury.com/eng/publicaciones/PDF/Civil/CI_09.pdf> last accessed 3 December 2013

MERCIECA, A (1954): 'Sir Adriano Dingli: sommo statista, legislatore, magistrato' in *Melita Historica* Malta Historical Society 1(1954) 3, Malta

ONUFRIO, MV (2004): 'Harmonisation of European contract law and legal translation: a role for comparative lawyers' in Indret 2(2004) *Revista para el Análisis del Derecho*

POZZO, B (2003): 'Harmonisation of European Contract Law and the Need of Creating a Common Terminology' in 6 (2003) *European Review of Private Law*

Other materials

RUET, C (1998-99) *La résiliation unilatérale des contrats à exécution successive* Unpublished thesis, Université Paris XI, Paris n° 172

Liber Bestiarum, Manuscript 764 at the Bodleian Library, University of Oxford, United Kingdom

Legislative materials

Les Coutumes du Pais et Duché d'Angoumois, Aunis et Gouvernement de la Rochelle (1720) Rezé & Puinesge, Angouleme

Code Napoleon, or, The French Civil Code. Literally Translated from the Original and Official Edition, Published at Paris, in 1804. By a Barrister of the Inner Temple (1827) William Benning, Law Bookseller, London

Coûtumes Générales du Païs et Duché de Bretagne et Usemens Locaux de la Mesme Province (1746), Guillaume Vatar, Arennes

Repertorio Universale della Legislazione pel Regno d'Italia dall'Anno 1802 a tutto l'Anno 1809 (1811) Tomo IV P–R, Giovanni Parolari, Venice

Sentences

Causa Lanari e Rinaldi de Iorca, decided on 12 April 1834 (Decision XLIII), in L CANTINI, L (1835): *Tesoro del Foro Toscano ossia Raccolta delle Decisioni del Supremo Consiglio e delle Regie Ruote Civili delle Prime Appellazioni di Toscana* Tipografia del Giglio, Florence

Latin Wine Decanted into a Semitic Carafe: The Obscure Term "*Midheb*" in Vassalli's *Lexicon* and its Possible Usefulness for the Legal Historian

Books

Al-Mawrid Arabic-English Dictionary (2005) Dar El-Ilm Lilmalayin, Beirut

AQUILINA, J (1987): *Maltese-English Dictionary*, Vol. I, Midsea, Valletta

AZOPARDI, V (1856/2009): *Piccolo Dizionario* Għaqda tal-Malti – Università, Malta

BELLOMO, M (1995) (TRS. COCHRANE, L): *The Common Legal Past of Europe 1000-1800* The Catholic University of America Press, Washington D.C

CALASSO, F (1954): *Medioevo del diritto*, I Le Fonti, Milan

CARACAUSI, G (1930): *Arabismi Medievali di Sicilia* Centro di Studi Filologici e Linguistici Siciliani, Palermo

CAVANNA, A (1982): *Storia del diritto moderno in Europa: Le fonti e il pensiero giuridico* Giuffrè editore, Milan

CARABOTT, R (2016): *Damma Tal Kliem Karataginis mscerred fel Fom tal Maltin u Ghaucin Gianfrangesku Agius Sultana Ghauci* Akkademja tal-Malta *et al*, Malta

CHIARELLI, L (2010): *A History of Muslim Sicily* Midsea Books, Malta

CIAPPARA, F (2006): *Enlightenment and Reform in Malta 1740-1798* Midsea Books, Malta

CORRIENTE, F (1997): *A Dictionary of Andalusi Arabic* Brill, The Netherlands

DE BONO, P (1897): *Sommario della Storia della Legislazione in Malta* Tipografia del Malta, Valletta

DINGLI, A (1893): *On the Force and Effects of Custom (Consuetudo) According to the Civil (Roman) Law* E. Laferla, Malta

Encyclopaedia Judaica (1971) Keter Publishing, Jersualem Vol. 7

FIORINI, S (ED.) (1996): *Documentary Sources of Maltese History Part I: Notarial Documents No 1: Notary Giacomo Zabara R 494/1(I): 1486-1488* University of Malta Press, Malta

GROSSI, P (1995): *L'Ordine Giuridico Medievale* Laterza, Bari-Rome

---------- (2010) (TRS. L. HOOPER): *A History of European Law* Wiley-Blackwell, Chichester, United Kingdom

HALLAQ, W B (1997): *History of Islamic Legal Theories* Cambridge University Press, Cambridge

-------------- (2005): *The Origins and Evolution of Islamic Law* Cambridge University Press, Cambridge

-------------- (2009): *An Introduction to Islamic Law* Cambridge University Press, Cambridge

HECHT, N S ET AL.(ED.) (1996): *An Introduction to the History and Sources of Jewish Law* Oxford University Press, Oxford

LESAFFER, R (2009): *European Legal History: A Cultural and Political Perspective* (Cambridge University Press, Cambridge

MICALLEF, A (1841): *Dritto Municipale di Malta compilato sotto De Rohan G.M. Or Nuovamente Corredato di Annotazioni* Cumbo, Malta

MIFSUD, M (1995):, *Loan Verbs in Maltese: A Descriptive and Comparative Study* Brill, The Netherlands

PATRICK GLENN, H (2010): *Legal Traditions of the World* (4th ed.), Oxford University Press, Oxford

REIFFENSTUEL, A (1700; 1834 ed.): *Jus canonicum universum* Dominicum Ercole, Rome

RICHERI, T M (1792): *Dictionarium Juris Civilis, Canonici et Feudalis nec non delectus legum feudalium* Ex Typographia regia, Turin

SAMMUT, F (1995): *Il-Ħolma Maltija* SKS, Malta

------------ (2009): *Introduction to Azopardi's Piccolo Dizionario* Għaqda tal-Malti – Università, Malta

SERRACINO INGLOTT, E (1979): *Il-Miklem Malti* Klabb Kotba Maltin, Malta

SICILIANO-VILLANUEVA, L (1901/1986): *Sul Diritto Greco-Romano Privato in Sicilia* Arnaldo Forni Editore, Sala Bolognese, Palermo

THESAN, CAV (c. 1600/1999): *Maltese-Italian dictionary* Mons. Lawrenz Cachia, Malta

VASSALLI, M A (1796/2002): *Ktŷb yl Klŷm Mâlti 'Mfysser Byl-Latĭn u Byt-Taljân* Rome; SKS, Malta

----------------- (1828/2006): *Motti, Aforismi e Proverbii maltesi* Malta; Argo, Malta

VICAT, PH (1759) *Vocabularium Juris Utrisque* Bousquetania, Naples

WETTINGER, G (2006): *Kliem Malti Qadim* Istitut tal-Lingwistika, Università ta' Malta, Malta

ZIMMERMANN, R (2001): *Roman Law, Contemporary Law, European Law: The Civilian Tradition Today* Oxford University Press, Oxford

Chapters in books

BIROCCHI, I (2006): 'La Formazione dei Diritti Patrî nell'Europa Moderna tra Politica dei Sovrani e Pensiero Giuspolitico, Prassi ed Insegnamento' in BIROCCHI, I & MATTONE, A (EDS.) *Il diritto patrio: tra diritto comune e codificazione (secoli XVI-XIX)* Viella, Rome

FIORINI, S (1999): "*Ut Vulgo Dicitur*: Pre-1600 Materials for a Documented Etymology of Maltese" in XUEREB, P (ED.) *Karissime Gotifride: Historical essays presented to Godfrey Wettinger on his seventieth birthday* Malta University Press, Malta

LAZARUS-YAFEH, H (1979): 'Judeo-Arabic culture' in ROTH, C (ED.) *Encyclopaedia Judaica Yearbook 1977/78* Keter Publishing House Ltd, Jerusalem

PENNINGTON, K (2008): "*Lex Naturalis* and *Ius Naturalis*" in *The Jurist* 68 University of Pittsburgh, Pittsburgh

PINZINO, J M (2003): "Joan of Arc and the *Lex Privata*: A Spirit of Freedom in the Law" in ASTELL, A W & WHEELER, B (EDS.) *Joan of Arc and Spirituality*, Palgrave Macmillan, New York

PIZZORUSSO, A (1997): 'Pluralismo delle fonti interne' in *Storia d'Italia (Annali 14): Legge Diritto Giustizia* Einaudi Editore, Turin

Articles in journals

BALOSSINO, S (2005): "Iustitita, lex, consuetudo: per un vocabolario della giustizia nei capitolari italici", *Reti Medievali Rivista*, VI - 2005/1 (January-June) <http://www.dssg.unifi .it/_RM/rivista/saggi/Balossino.htm> (Firenze University Press, Florence 2005) accessed 12/08/2012

DU PLESSIS, P J (2006): "The Roman Concept of lex contractus", 3 *Roman Legal Trad.* Roman Law Society of America, at the University of Kansas School of Law, Lawrence, Kansas

JACOBSON, A J (2005): "Publishing Dissent", 62 *Wash. & Lee L. Rev.* Washington and Lee University, Lexington, Virgina

MAKDISI, J A (1998-99): "The Islamic Origins of the Common Law", 77 N.C. L. Rev. The University of North Carolina at Chapel Hill, Chapel Hill, North Carolina

POTZ, R (2011): "Islam and Islamic Law in European Legal History" in *European History Online* (EGO) (Institute of European History (IEG), Mainz 2011-11-21). URL: http://www.ieg-ego.eu/potzr-2011a-en URN: urn:nbn:de:0159-2011112112 [2012-07-12]

RICH, P B (1998): "Racial ideas and the impact of imperialism in Europe" in *The European Legacy: Toward New Paradigms*, Vol. 3, No. 1, pp. 31-44 Routledge, London

SERRANO, D (2000): "Legal Practice in an Andalusī-Maghribī Source from the Twelfth Century CE: The Madhāhib Al-ḥukkām fī Nawāzil al-Aḥkām", *Islamic L. & Soc'y* 187 Brill, The Netherlands

SCHACHT, J (1950): "Foreign Elements in Ancient Islamic Law", *Journal of Comparative Legislation and International Law*, Third Series, Vol. 32, No. 3/4 Cambridge University Press on behalf of the British Institute of International and Comparative Law, Cambridge

ZIMMERMAN, R (2007): "Roman Law and European Culture", *New Zealand Law Review* 341 Legal Research Foundation, Auckland, New Zealand

Other materials

FSADNI, R (2011): "Did Breivik have a point?" in *The Times* Allied Newspapers, Malta 28 July 2011

Index

www.ingramcontent.com/pod-product-compliance
Lightning Source LLC
LaVergne TN
LVHW101504200926
848483LV00001B/222
* 9 7 8 1 9 1 2 1 4 2 0 1 9 *